WILDCAT STRIKE

harper 🔥 torchbooks

A reference-list of Harper Torchbooks, classified by subjects, is printed at the end of this volume.

RESEARCHES IN THE SOCIAL, CULTURAL AND BEHAVIORAL SCIENCES

edited by BENJAMIN NELSON

Alfred Adler	PROBLEMS OF NEUROSIS, edited by H. L. Ansbacher. TB/1145
Gladys Bryson	*MAN AND SOCIETY: *The Scottish Inquiry of the Eighteenth Century.*
Kenelm Burridge	*MAMBU: *A Melanesian Millennium*
Allison Davis and John Dollard	CHILDREN OF BONDAGE: *The personality development of Negro youth in the Urban South.* TB/3049
Emile Durkheim, et al.	ESSAYS ON SOCIOLOGY AND PHILOSOPHY, *with appraisals of Durkheim's life and work,* edited by Kurt H. Wolff. TB/1151
Leon Festinger, Henry W. Riecken and Stanley Schachter	WHEN PROPHECY FAILS: *A social and psychological study of a modern group that predicted the destruction of the world.* TB/1132
Herbert Fingarette	THE SELF IN TRANSFORMATION: *Psychoanalysis, Philosophy and the Life of the Spirit.* TB/1177
Raymond Firth, editor	MAN AND CULTURE: *An evaluation of the work of Bronislaw Malinowski.* TB/1133
Alvin W. Gouldner	WILDCAT STRIKE: *A Study in Worker-Management Relationships.* TB/1176
J. L. Hammond	*THE RISE OF MODERN INDUSTRY, Introduction by Max Hartwell
J. L. and Barbara Hammond	*THE TOWN LABORER
	*THE VILLAGE LABORER
David Landy	*TROPICAL CHILDHOOD: *Cultural Transmission and Learning in a Rural Puerto Rican Village*
Kurt Lewin	FIELD THEORY IN SOCIAL SCIENCE: *Selected Theoretical Papers,* edited by Dorwin Cartwright. TB/1135
David Lockwood	*THE BLACK-COATED WORKER
Robert K. Merton, Leonard Broom, Leonard S. Cottrell, Jr., editors	SOCIOLOGY TODAY: *Problems and Prospects.* Vol. I, TB/1173; Vol. II, TB/1174
John H. Rohrer and Munro S. Edmonson, editors	THE EIGHTH GENERATION GROWS UP: *Culture and Personalities of New Orleans Negroes.* TB/3050
Henri de Saint-Simon	SOCIAL ORGANIZATION, THE SCIENCE OF MAN, *and other writings,* edited by Felix Markham. TB/1152
Kurt Samuelsson	RELIGION AND ECONOMIC ACTION: *A Critique of Max Weber's* The Protestant Ethic and The Spirit of Capitalism. TB/1131
John H. Schaar	ESCAPE FROM AUTHORITY: *The perspectives of* Erich Fromm. TB/1155
Muzafer Sherif	*GROUP RELATIONS AT THE CROSSROADS
	*THE PSYCHOLOGY OF SOCIAL NORMS
Georg Simmel, et al.	*GEORG SIMMEL: 1858-1918; *Translations from his writings and essays on his thought,* edited by Kurt H. Wolff.
Ernest Lee Tuveson	MILLENNIUM AND UTOPIA: *A Study in the Background of the Idea of Progress.* TB/1134
W. Lloyd Warner	A BLACK CIVILIZATION: *A Study of an Australian Tribe.* TB/3056
W. Lloyd Warner and Associates	DEMOCRACY IN JONESVILLE: *A Study in Quality and Inequality.* TB/1129

**in preparation*

WILDCAT STRIKE

A Study in Worker-Management Relationships

by

Alvin W. Gouldner

HARPER TORCHBOOKS / *The Academy Library*

HARPER & ROW, PUBLISHERS

NEW YORK, EVANSTON AND LONDON

TO
HELEN SATTLER GOULDNER

WILDCAT STRIKE

Printed in the United States of America.
This book was originally published in 1954
by The Antioch Press, and is here reprinted by arrangement.
First HARPER TORCHBOOK edition published 1965 by
Harper & Row, Publishers, Incorporated,
49 East 33rd Street, New York, New York 10016.
Library of Congress catalog card number: 54-6176.

Preface

THIS IS THE SECOND REPORT on our gypsum studies and is, as such, the companion piece to *Patterns of Industrial Bureaucracy*.[1] The present volume has, however, been prepared in a manner enabling it to be read independently of the first.

I should like to express my deep appreciation to the *Social Science Research Council*, and to its executive associate Mr. Elbridge Sibley, for two grants which greatly facilitated the completion of this study. The first of these was an appointment to the Council's seminar on "Leadership and Small Group Behavior" held at Dartmouth College in the summer of 1952. My co-participants in this seminar, Bernard Bass, Cecil Gibb, John Hemphill, Seymour M. Lipset, and Ben Willerman did much to stimulate the thinking that went into this report. A second award in 1953 provided an opportunity to complete the write-up of the study. On both occasions, the excellent facilities of Baker Library at Dartmouth College were generously made available through the good offices of G. H. Gliddon.

Those familiar with the seminal thinking of Robert K. Merton will recognize at a glance the variety and depth of our obligation to him. Indeed, it was at Mr. Merton's encouragement that I undertook to prepare this study for publication. I am, also, gratefully aware of the insight I have derived from the studies of other social scientists and, particularly, from Talcott Parsons, John R. Commons, Max Weber, and Sigmund Freud. That I have nowhere felt a need to engage in the mere exegesis of their work, but have sought only to use it in attacking new problems is, perhaps, still another indication of the vitality of their ideas.

There is a special debt that I owe to my friend and former de-

[1] Free Press, 1954. Since our methods of investigation are reported in the appendix to this study, I have not felt it necessary to review them again in the present volume.

partment chairman, Nathaniel Cantor, whose administrative wisdom made it possible for me to integrate roles as a teacher and researcher. At many points, other friends and former colleagues at the University of Buffalo helped substantially with technical advice. Among these are Llewellyn Z. Gross, Milton C. Albrecht, Norman Miller, Jack Hyman, and Joseph Shister. More recently, I have had the benefit of very helpful consultations with Glen Heathers of the Fels Research Institute, and with Erling Eng and Everett K. Wilson of Antioch College. Intensive discussions with Maurice R. Stein of Oberlin College were particularly valuable in developing the final chapters on the rudiments of a general theory of group tensions.

I am deeply appreciative, also, to former students at the University of Buffalo who contributed greatly to this project through their interviewing and in other ways. Among these, I might especially mention Phyllis Herrick Hartell, Dolores Paul, Lois W. Hoffman, Harold Bershady, Gunnar Hanson, and Karl Girshman. Freeman Champney, manager of the Antioch Press, has proved an ideal publisher, wise in editorial counsel and knowledgeable concerning many of the problems with which this study attempts to deal. Finally, the continued cooperation of both the men and the management of the "General Gypsum Company," even during the travail of the strike, was an indispensable condition for the successful conduct of the research.

The diagrams in the ninth and tenth chapters are the artwork of Antioch's Walter Severson and we are appreciative of his creative pictorialization of our ideas.

It is needless to add, I am sure, that responsibility for the shortcomings of this study is entirely the author's.

A. W. G.
May, 1954
Yellow Springs, Ohio

Table of Contents

Chapter One

INTRODUCTION

THIS IS A STUDY of an industrial conflict, a "wildcat strike," which took place in a plant owned and operated by the General Gypsum Company.[1]

The following account seeks to realize several objectives. Our most general intention is to present the facts of the case and to describe in some detail the events that occurred. This is especially needful since there are few descriptions of wildcat strikes written from a sociologist's viewpoint. Indeed, so little attention has been given to this form of industrial conflict that it is not entirely clear what the term "wildcat strike" means; usually, only the most general allusions to its "spontaneous" and unplanned character are made. At some point, therefore, it will become necessary to ask, just what is a "wildcat strike," and how does it differ from other types of strikes? Such conceptual clarification is a second objective of this study, and is a necessary preliminary to the explanation of what happened.

We shall want to know how this strike came about: Did the parties expect it? Did they want it? What did they do to prevent it? How did the belief systems and social relations of workers and management enter into the events that occurred? In other words, we are not in the least interested here in who was "right" and who "wrong." So far as it can be accomplished, the basic task is one of disciplined examination rather than of moral condemnation.

The final objective, however, is not simply the explanation of this one strike but, instead, the development of hypotheses and conceptual tools which can illuminate other similar processes. In short,

---

[1] All proper names are pseudonyms, used to protect the anonymity of the Company and its personnel.

it is possible that the careful examination of this one case may provide occasions to test and develop instruments of more general application to industrial sociology and to a theory of group tensions.

Social scientists of the most varying standpoints agree that human action can be rendered meaningful only by relating it to the contexts in which it takes place. The meaning and consequences of a behavior pattern will vary with the contexts in which it occurs. This is commonly recognized in the saying that there is a "time and a place for everything."

There should be no implication, however, that the social scientist is a sort of "happy savage" who has merely to reach out his hand to pluck these "contexts" from some tree of knowledge, where they hang waiting to edify him. The social scientist does not passively encounter or discover the contexts he uses as tools, but actively creates and selects them. Such a selection is necessary because the contexts in which events take place can never be dealt with in their complete detail. As a sociologist, this writer is inevitably more familiar and competent with the contexts traditionally studied by his discipline, and these, of course, will be drawn upon more frequently than, though not to the complete exclusion of, standpoints employed by other behavioral sciences.

But if we cannot understand events without framing them within a context, neither can we decide which contexts will be helpful in accounting for behavior without clarifying the behavior involved. Thus the social scientist is usually engaged in two closely connected operations at the same time, namely, the job of locating, sifting out, and clarifying behavior patterns that interest him and, simultaneously, the task of selecting, refining, and building interpretative contexts. In the chapters that follow, these two tasks will be treated in alternating succession, the behavioral problem and the explanatory contexts each undergoing progressive clarification and refinement.

The Community Context

Oscar Center, the town in which the plant is located, has about 700 residents and is situated some sixteen miles from Lakeport. This is a middle-sized city near the Great Lakes, in which the Company's main office is located. Most of the men working in the plant live in Oscar Center or in Oscar, Pinefield, West House, Tyre, or Beeville, which are on the periphery of Lakeport's metropolitan area. Each of these towns is less than 5,000 in population.

Oscar Center, in many ways representative of the other communities, is predominantly composed of people of Germanic origin and of Lutheran or Catholic religion. Formerly, the Lutheran Church gave one sermon a month in German, but this practice has now been discontinued. It is a rather prim community in which dancing, for example, is still frowned upon by certain of the elders. Like most of the nearby communities, it belongs to a softball league which was started by a former head of the Lutheran Church, and the townsmen take a keen interest in the local team. Another important source of recreation and sociability for many people are the meetings and card parties of the Volunteer Fire Department, which also supports a drum and bugle corps.

Family life in Oscar Center is dominated by men; as one respondent said, "The old man is boss, and the women are submissive." And further, "The feuds that exist, exist between families. There has rarely been a divorce out here. The families are quite interlocked by marriage." The men are avid coon hunters in their spare time. The women can only "get out on Saturday nights." If not tending to their household chores, they may visit with their neighbors or do some sewing at the church. Though the town is near Lakeport, children often do not visit this city until they are of high school age, since their parents feel that it is too big and noisy.

Social status in the town depends greatly on length of residence; "many families have been here for 25 years and are still considered newcomers." Thus at the bottom of the social ladder are the new arrivals. At the top, two groups are to be found: (1) the old, established farm families, and (2) the few professionals such as the doctor and ministers. In addition to being ranked socially in terms of their community seniority, the inhabitants are also graded in terms of their occupation, whether or not they possess the prized independence of farm-holdings, and their moral rectitude.

Though most townsmen are engaged in non-farming occupations, they are still farm-oriented, either owning or living on a farm, or aspiring to do so. Many of the men work at the Oscar Center plant because it is near them, rather than take a daily ride to Lakeport. Being among their families and friends, living in their own homes and in the familiar neighborhoods of their birth are salient values to these people. Supervisors and workers have thus often grown up together and know each other's families. As a result, they have developed friendly informal ties which are reinforced by such jointly shared activities as bowling, drinking together, hunting, and fishing.

Like other members of small communities, the men at the Oscar Center plant focus their loyalties on local institutions. Insofar as the Company is concerned, much of their aggression is focussed on the Lakeport main office, which they blame for changes they dislike, rather than on local management.

So far as their union is concerned, the workers' loyalty is largely to their own local of the Gas, Coke and Chemical Workers, CIO. The workers' feelings toward those in the upper regions of the union hierarchy are a mixture of hostility and suspicion. In fact, when the Union's national officers removed their regional representative, whom they accused of being a Communist, the workers in the plant—predominantly Republican voters themselves—rallied to his defense almost to a man. The workers' complaints about their former A.F. of L. union express a similar localism; their major grievance against it was that its main office was too far away to be of any help.

This description of the community is a static one and has neglected, thus far, to indicate the trends toward increasing urbanization which were being manifested. By World War I, many farmers began to move into industry, earning their livelihoods as wage workers. The depression of 1929 further accentuated this when some of the local railroads stopped hauling freight and made farming impossible for many who had wished to continue it. World War II brought still more men, largely those beyond draft age, off their farms into factories.

Canning, gypsum, paper, and other light industries moved into the countryside and took root. The farms became increasingly mechanized; farmers retired their horses and took to tractors and all kinds of mechanical loaders, balers, and silage apparatus. The increased use of machinery, in turn, made farmers less socially dependent on each other, for there was now less necessity to exchange turns helping each other out.

Wartime speculation in land brought in strange faces, making it less likely that the farmer next door would be known. Under the pressure of increasingly evident economic distinctions, the former community cohesiveness began to give way. Occasionally, the different groups would conduct a social tug of war for control of the Volunteer Fire Department, membership in which became increasingly honorific and "exclusive." Those living on the "better" side of town began to play bridge and to join the Masons. The younger people were "not the craftsmen their fathers were" and they began to scatter to the cities in larger numbers. In short, with the transformation of farming into a business, class stratification in the town emerged more clearly, and intimate personalized relationships began to wane. But while the community was certainly less rural than it used to be, it was still very far from being maturely urbanized.

The Plant

The factory itself is but half an hour's ride from the northern rim of Lakeport. The plant's two basic divisions are the sub-surface mining and the surface factory processing operations. In 1948, there were about 225 people employed, 75 in the mine and 150 in various surface departments. Most people at the plant worked a six day week, eight hours a day; their wages were computed on the basis of a forty hour week, with time and a half for overtime.

The central item in the flow of operations is gypsum rock. This is first blasted out of the walls of mining rooms, about eighty or so feet beneath the surface. It is then scooped up by great mechanical lobsters, the "joy-loaders," piled onto "shuttle buggies," which carry it to trains waiting nearby. The trains bring the roughly hewn "gyp" to the "foot" (or rear) of the mine where it is weighed and crushed into more manageable chunks. If the rock is used immediately, instead of being stored or shipped elsewhere, it is pulverized into a fine powder and dehydrated, a process known as "calcining."

In this form, the gypsum may be used either as a main ingredient for wall plaster or, as most of it is used, to make gypsum wall board. For this purpose, the powder is conveyed to the "board" building which is the center of all surface activities. Here it is fed into a mixer, along with other ingredients, and is churned into a paste.

This is poured onto a moving sheet of paper, and is at first somewhat smoothed down by hand. It passes between two rotating cylinders which compress it to a desired thickness, cover it with a top sheet, and seal its edges. As a continuous strip of board, several hundreds of feet long, it is conveyed over rollers slowly enough to set partially before it reaches a mechanical knife. Near the end of the rollers, it is cut into sections of variable length and rolled onto alternate decks of a multi-tiered steam heated dryer, through which it passes in about an hour. Upon emerging from the dryer, the board is inspected, bundled, and loaded at the "take-off" point.

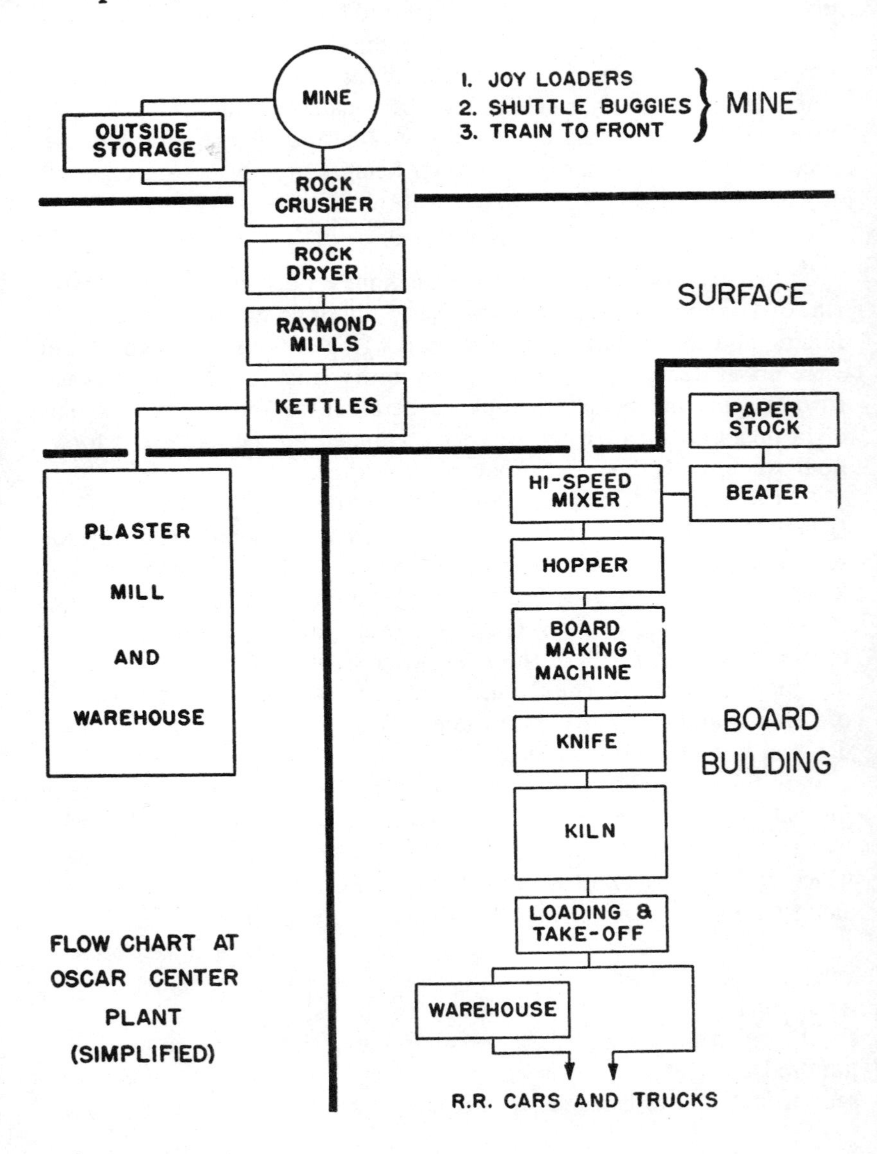

FLOW CHART AT OSCAR CENTER PLANT (SIMPLIFIED)

From about 1948 to 1951, about $1,500,000 in new equipment was installed in the board building. In particular, the old board machine and kiln were replaced, though the equipment at the take-off end remained unchanged. The objective of these changes was, of course, to increase the speed and economy with which the board could be produced.

Two other important divisions of the plant deserve mention here. The first consists of maintenance activities, the bulk of which are localized in the repair shop on the surface. There is also another repair shop down in the mine, since it is difficult to bring the bulky mine machinery to the top when it breaks down.

There is, also, the office building where the plant manager's and personnel director's offices are located, the records stored, payroll preparations made, and communications with the Lakeport office maintained. The office building stands noticeably apart from the cluster of dusty production units and, during the summer, is bordered with a bed of flowers which further marks it off from the dinginess of the other buildings.

Worker-Management Relationships

At the peak of the authority system in the plant there was the Plant Manager, who was subordinate only to the main office executives in Lakeport. In practice, this meant that the executives in the main office Production Department were his effective superiors in most matters, except those of personnel administration which was under the jurisdiction of the Labor Relations Department in Lakeport. Directly beneath the plant manager were two key "staff" officers, the "office manager," and the "personnel and safety manager." The "line" command, also under the plant manager, consisted, first, of the supervisors of the key buildings and divisions, for example, the head of the board building, and the mill, maintenance, and mine superintendents. Under each of these there were, in turn, a number of foremen who had direct and continual contact with a small group of workers.

It will be assumed here, provisionally, that the stability of worker-management relationships ordinarily rested on a set of shared expectations which the men in one group had concerning their own rights and privileges, and the degree to which those in the other group

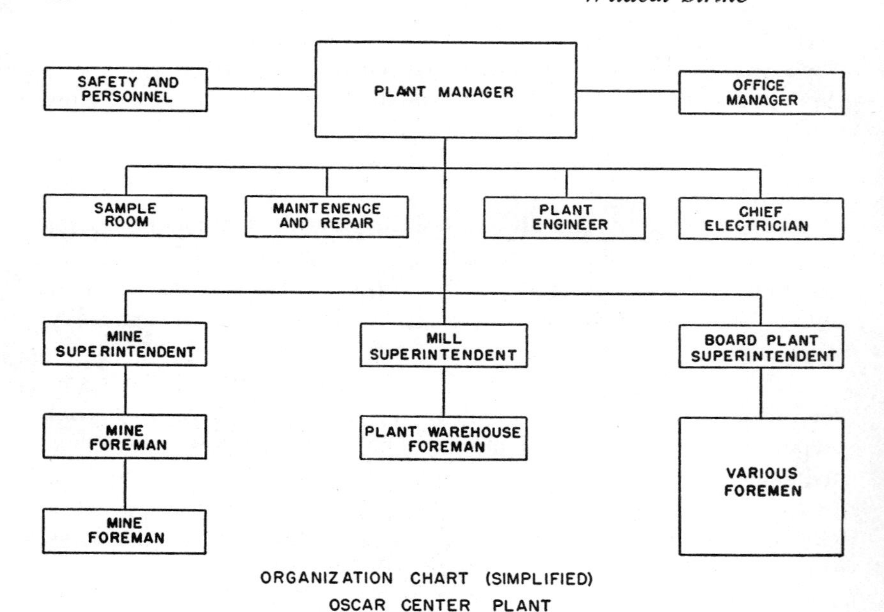

ORGANIZATION CHART (SIMPLIFIED)
OSCAR CENTER PLANT

conformed to these expectations in their daily activities. Specifically, what did the Oscar Center workers expect of their foremen and supervisors? One of the first things to be noted is that these expectations had varying degrees of saliency, some of them being in the forefront of the workers' attention and frequently expressed, while others were rarely expressed at all.

The Indulgency Pattern

In a word, a word frequently used by the workers themselves, their most salient expectation was "leniency," which in itself can be analyzed into a number of concrete, component expectations. Very importantly, most workers expected that they were there "to do a job," and that there should be "no constant check-up on you," and "when there's work to do they expect you to do it, but otherwise they leave you alone." In short, workers defined their main role obligation as working or producing. Their obedience obligations to superiors were residual or auxiliary; at best these were thought of as legitimate demands only insofar as they were necessary to do a particular job.

When work took place under close supervision, or when workers felt that discipline was being exerted for its own sake or merely as a way of asserting the superiority of management, they resented it and became hostile to their superiors and apathetic about their work.

A second expectancy shared by the workers, one quite similar to the Roman notion of "clemency" and the feudal conception of "noblesse oblige," was that of the "second chance." Thus the Company was praised because of its readiness to rehire men who had quit to take better paying jobs elsewhere during the war boom. The men commended supervisors who warned workers before firing them, and who listened to "reasonable" excuses for lateness, instead of seizing every opportunity to inflict a punishment. Closely related to this "second chance" element was the appreciation which workers expressed of management when the latter behaved flexibly with regard to plant rules. For example, when workers were allowed to punch in a little earlier, if they wanted to make some extra money by accumulating overtime, and occasionally, when they were allowed to punch out early, if they had something special to do in the evening, they commented favorably about management's "leniency." Clearly, here was a built-in source of flexibility in worker-management relations, allowing adaptation to the peculiarities of each individual case. It was a device of flexibility, however, usable only at the discretion of management.

Another expectancy shared by the workers provided them with an area of discretion useful in controlling management behavior. This was the "job shifting" expectation which said, in effect, that workers should have opportunities to change their jobs within the plant, either vertically or horizontally. This was incorporated in the union-management contract and referred to as the "bidding" clause.

Nominally, job shifting, by "bidding" for a new vacancy, was a means of attaining upward social mobility. In actuality, however, job shifting was also important as a way of escaping from an unpleasant foreman. Unless a supervisor "played ball," workers could take a job under some other foreman. When a worker bid for and got a job in some other building or division of the plant, no "favors" had been done and no obligations had been incurred to a foreman, thus narrowing the supervisors' and foremen's discretionary powers. In part for this reason, some of the foremen resented the contractual provision for job shifting and sought to evade it; they still tended to conceive of themselves as having some right to choose their own subordinates.

A fourth expectancy that workers had of their superiors was somthing that might be called "protection," particularly in matters of physical welfare. Workers in the plant, and especially the miners who worked under more hazardous conditions, believed that it was a foreman's obligation to maintain safe working conditions and expected the Company to "take care of them" in the event of an injury while at work. The manner in which the Company treated a disabled worker was a significant yardstick, widely referred to by workers in explaining what they meant by Company "leniency."

Since the Company was legally compelled to compensate a worker, in the event of a disabling accident on the job, the workers looked to other expressions of the Company's attitude toward the injured. They especially commended the Company for not requiring the injured worker to stay at home, and for allowing him to work in the "sample room," where the work was light and could be done while sitting. Here the injured worker, who was unable to return to his regular job, might earn a higher income than he would from accident compensation.

A fifth indication of what workers meant by "leniency" is found in references to "government jobs," i.e., the use of Company equipment and material for home repairs. Workers expected that they would have preferential access to the Company's finished product, that they could get gypsum board without charge or at a very large discount, and that they could use plant equipment and material to repair broken farm machinery or household furnishings.

Here, then, were five expectations of managerial behavior held by workers which, when complied with by management, were spoken of as "leniency." To facilitate reference to them, we have called this the "indulgency pattern." It should be evident that these do not comprise the totality of the workers' shared expectations, and that there were other things they desired of management. For example, workers valued "seniority," and expected that management would give special consideration to those who had been at the plant longest. Thus the indulgency pattern is a selection from a larger battery of worker expectations.

In this respect the indulgency pattern may be conceived of as the counterpart to the informal social code which Roethlisberger and

Dickson identified in their studies of workers at the Western Electric Company.[2] The latter code, however, primarily referred to and regulated the relations between worker and worker, that is, the expectations workers directed toward each other. The indulgency pattern, however, focusses on the worker's expectations of *managerial* personnel. Like the indulgency pattern, however, it is obvious that the Western Electric informal code is only a partial description of worker expectations, though with regard to a different relationship.

The selection of expectations to comprise the indulgency pattern was not an arbitrary one; for all the elements in it are particularly salient, referring to things reiterated by the workers themselves, and to which workers explicitly attributed significance as a source of their job satisfaction. Thus the indulgency pattern was a distinctively important factor motivating workers to fill the roles for which they had been employed, expressing a commitment to a set of beliefs as to how the plant should be run, and generating loyalties to the Company and management. While other elements also influenced work motivation, those in the indulgency pattern were at the center of the workers' daily attention and comprised the standards they most commonly used to judge the plant.

There were further ways in which the expectations incorporated in the indulgency pattern differed from others held by workers. It may be observed that workers did not define management as "lenient" when the latter gave "tit for tat." Specifically, workers did not tend to speak of "leniency" when they were given something that they already felt to be rightfully theirs. Instead, this approving judgment was reserved for management behavior which complied with expectations of tenuous legitimacy, and when management gave up something for which workers could make no compelling claim.

For example, workers never commended management, or spoke of its "leniency," when they were paid their proper wages; it is, in

---

[2] F. J. Roethlisberger and W. J. Dickson, with the collaboration of H. A. Wright, *Management and the Worker,* Harvard University Press, Cambridge, Mass., 1946. This study indicated that workers held such beliefs as: you must restrict production to an amount which had been informally agreed upon; you must not produce too far below this amount; you must not act like a "big shot," and as if you were better than other workers.

part, for this reason that wage satisfactions are not an element in the indulgency pattern. On the other hand, management would be within its *legal rights* if it kept workers busy every minute of the time for which they were being paid. Insofar as management did *not* do so, workers spoke of it as lenient.

The case of the sample room, and its use as the factory "hospital," further illustrates this. Management did not have to allow injured workers to earn money at the jobs in the sample room; it could have insisted that injured workers remain at home, collecting their compensation only, until they were ready to resume their regular jobs. But, here again, the Company did not "stand on its rights."

Similarly, management was not compelled to allow workers to punch in early, or to punch out early; nor was it required to allow workers to use Company materials for household repairs. It was, however, primarily in these situations, when the Company did not appear to strive for a return on every cost, for a gain against every outlay, when management did what it was privileged not to do, that workers felt it to have a "proper attitude," and said they were being treated "humanly."

It is clear, then, that workers did not define "leniency" as a management *obligation*. Instead, "leniency" seems to refer to managerial compliances with workers' role preferences, rather than role prescriptions. Furthermore, "leniency" also involves managerial behavior which is tempered by taking into account the worker's obligations in his other roles, for example, his obligations as a family member to maintain the family's income, to fix broken things around the house, or to leave work early to take "the wife" on a special outing.

In other words, when workers judged the plant to be "lenient," they were utilizing standards that would be relevant in some other situation or relationship, criteria legitimately applicable to the relations among family members, friends, or neighbors. The "second chance" expectation is a clear indication of this. These expectations, however, were only of dubious validity in a *business* and *industrial* context, and it is in part for this reason that management's compliance with them was especially noted and commended. In sum, the expectancies incorporated in the indulgency pattern were a problematic part of the workers' total role expectations, differing from others which had a firm and unambiguous legitimacy.

Tensions and Defenses

Other than providing a partial description of workers' beliefs, which may have general value in later accounting for the events of the wildcat strike, what gains accrue from an understanding of the indulgency pattern? For one thing, identification of the shared expectations comprising the indulgency pattern concomitantly indicates some of the kinds of behavior by which workers will be frustrated. Knowing what the workers like, it is possible to predict what they will dislike. Knowing, in short, the managerial actions that generate worker satisfaction and stabilize the relationship between the two, there is a basis for expecting that the contrary behaviors will elicit dissatisfactions among workers and create tensions in their relationships with management.

Secondly, the indulgency pattern's role in engendering worker-management tensions is easily neglected, for there exists a culturally standardized explanation of such conflicts which stresses the significance of economic dissatisfactions and deprivations. In short, "wages and hours" are commonly assumed to be *adequate* reasons for industrial tension, rather than whether or not workers are subjected to "close supervision," or are denied a "second chance." By deliberately focussing on the indulgency pattern, a set of factors ordinarily overshadowed in the explanation of industrial tensions may be made accessible to systematic analysis.

This is not to say that the "wage issue" will be ignored in the analysis that follows, though it is certain that a sociologist is neither as competent nor as interested in assessing the importance of this factor as an economist. Insofar as the wage issue is to be examined here, however, it will not be treated as "the" factor inducing industrial tensions, but only as one among a number of closely interwoven elements. Nor will it be taken for granted that, "of course," workers are interested in their wages; instead, it will be useful to consider the conditions under which workers are *more* or *less* interested in wages. In dealing with this question, it will be found that the indulgency pattern has important connections with variations of workers' interest in wages and in the development of the wage issue.

A third basis for concern with the indulgency pattern is that it gives some indication of the saliency of different expectations which workers direct toward management. Strains may be expected to arise in worker-management relations, not merely when the two have contradictory expectations, but also when a significant expectation has a different importance ascribed to it by the different parties, so that one rates it higher than the other.

To consider a critical example: In one part of the indulgency pattern, it was indicated that workers defined their main role obligations to be that of "working" or "producing." Their "obedience" obligations, however, were not equally stressed, and tended to be treated as legitimate only insofar as necessary to "do a job." An incongruous example may clarify this: workers would have been amazed if, instead of being awakened in the morning with the call, "Time to go to work, dear," their wives called out, "Get up, dear, it's time to go to *obey.*"

In short, workers defined their role in relation to the technological system, emphasizing their production obligation, and their ties to an impersonal process, but neglected to define with equal clarity their role in the plant's authority system, their place in a hierarchy of human relations. They thus indicate that they expect their obedience obligations to be of secondary importance.

To management, also, "production comes first," at least in its formal definition of its role. Frequently, however, management finds itself in the position of giving orders whose relevance to production is not evident to the workers. Insofar as this happens, tensions arise between the two.

Usually, management operates with a conception of "managerial prerogatives," e.g., the right to determine what it will produce, at what prices and speed of production; underlying these is an assumption of its own right to command. Ordinarily, management does not rest its right to command on its fulfillment of production obligations alone. Without analyzing this further, perhaps enough has been said to suggest that management ascribes greater importance to obedience obligations than do workers, and that here there is a potentially important source of tension between the two.

A fourth significance of the indulgency pattern, in a study of industrial tensions, has to do with the peculiar character of the expectations which it incorporates, and, specifically, with the fact that these expectations are of tenuous legitimacy in an *industrial* situation. This is consequential in several ways. Insofar as a set of expectations is recognized, even by those who hold them, as of doubtful validity, their gratification is relatively unstable. Those on whom such claims are pressed may more readily and unpredictably resist them. Conversely, those who hold the expectations may not advance them with the conviction and unity of action that they would pursue a claim about which they had no doubt. Focussing as it does on expectations of dubious legitimacy, the indulgency pattern therefore identifies certain enduring areas of instability in worker-management relations, and brackets off some strategic points where breakdowns may begin.

Fifth, and finally, this non-legitimate aspect of the indulgency pattern is also consequential for the *kinds* of responses which workers will make when management fails to conform to these expectations. It interposes a barrier inhibiting certain types of responses and tends to channel workers' resistance into specific directions and forms.

For example, it becomes unlikely that violation of the indulgency pattern will result in efforts at contractual and union negotiated remedies. This does not mean, of course, that resentment springing from frustration of the workers' indulgency expectations will have no impact on contract demands and negotiations. What is suggested, though, is that it is improbable that these specific criteria of leniency—e.g., private use of Company tools—will become matters of contractual discussion if ignored by management. Contractual, or formal, solutions seem more definitely indicated when there have been violations of workers' expectations which had unmistakable legitimacy.

Such violations would allow the broadest solidarity among workers, facilitating concerted remedial action, and be most likely to enlist public support. On the other hand, the defense of non-legitimate expectations is more likely to promote cleavages among the workers themselves, and to expose them to public criticism. In short, even if the indulgency pattern is violated, it should not be expected to result in concerted and public efforts at redress, at least immediately.

Stated differently and more broadly, a "social problem" is unlikely to arise unless people feel that their *legitimate* expectations have been abused. This does not imply that there will be no frustration, no problem experienced by workers, should the indulgency pattern be violated. The frustration of expectations of dubious legitimacy generates what may be called a "latent problem," a problem characterized initially by informal and covert efforts at solution. It is a problem which is slower to come "to the surface," in the sense that the accumulated resentment is more likely to fester and is less readily communicated. It is marked, in short, by guerilla forays rather than by open declarations of war.

There is at least a second way in which the non-legitimacy of the indulgency pattern may affect workers' defense tactics. If, as suggested above, grievances concerning indulgency expectations will tend to be inhibited, then there is the possibility that these grievances will be displaced onto other issues, there to be given expression in covert form. Onto what other issue might grievances about indulgency expectations be displaced? One possibility presents itself immediately, namely, the wage issue; for the wage issue involves claims about which workers feel most fully confident. In a sense, a wage demand is always legitimate, and it is only a question of "how much?" The likelihood of such a displacement, from indulgency to wage grievances, is reinforced by other elements in the situation. First, the frustration of the indulgency pattern, which is being presumed here, closes down the possibilities of daily gratifications *on the job*; the chances of securing gratification in the working environment itself are being limited. Under such circumstances, wages would seem to become an increasingly important source of job satisfaction, one which can, moreover, be enjoyed outside of the plant.

Also disposing to the same result is the conception which workers share concerning the reasons for management's violation of the indulgency pattern. There is little doubt that most workers believed that when the Company behaved "badly," it did so out of pecuniary motives. They typically expressed this by calling the Company "cheap." One kiln worker, for example, a man who did not like the plant, saw its faults in this way:

> "What's wrong with this country and plant is the all-mighty dollar. This plant doesn't care about the men and the way they live, but only about 75% profit."

To the degree that a bad company is defined as one that "only gives a damn about money," then retaliation is likely to take the form of impairing the very pecuniary values that the company is believed to hold paramount; aggression will be directed at what is held to be "the root of the evil." It may, therefore, be expected that changes which violate the indulgency pattern will awaken increased pressure for wage demands.

Chapter Two

THE PURSUIT OF WAGES

AS THERE IS A PLACE FOR EVERYTHING, so, also, is there a time. And the time when these researches began, in 1948, was one of renewed postwar competition, for the gypsum industry as for others. Unlike the period during the war, the market was increasingly favorable to the buyer, while sellers had to exert themselves more energetically. The loss of job opportunities in defense plants, which were closed or closing down prior to the outbreak of the Korean War, also increased competition for jobs. Between 1948 and 1950, there was growing fear in the region about the possibilities of a general economic "recession." Production management at the Lakeport office began to speak of the need for changing the workers' "psychology," and of removing what they felt to be a war born laxness. They prepared, in their words, "to tighten things up and put the bit in the worker's mouth."

The occasion that precipitated this human relations retooling at the Oscar Center plant was the death of the old plant manager and the appointment of a new one, Vincent Peele. "Doug (the late manager) didn't force the machine," said Peele. "I had to watch it. Doug was satisfied with a certain production. *But the Company gave me orders to get production up.*"

From its very beginning, Peele's administration was marked by an increase in "strictness."[1] One of the earliest expressions of this was his dismissal of a miner. The man was fired for having taken some dynamite from the mine to use for fishing. In firing him, Peele

---

[1] In *Patterns of Industrial Bureaucracy*, we have examined Peele's behavior as a function of his needs and tensions as a "successor," i.e., as a new role occupant. These pressures coincided with the economic changes which played, as we emphasize here, an independent role in disposing him to "tighten up" the plant.

directly opposed the "government job" expectancies, under which the workers had traditionally helped themselves to all sorts of Company material, including dynamite.

Peele also contravened the workers' "second chance" expectancies, taking the attitude that he was going to "make an example" of this man. Shortly afterwards, he also dismissed the personnel and safety manager, who was an old plant employee, and brought in Digger, who had worked for Peele at the General Gypsum plant from which they both came.

Peele, further, required new daily and weekly reports from foremen and building superintendents, and increased restrictions on conversation groups, cutting down on the workers' "bull sessions." He also introduced restrictions that slowed down job-shifting. He installed a formal "warning notice," which was given to men for infraction of the rules, and which they had to acknowledge by signing.

Peele began to enforce the no-absenteeism rules strictly, punishing those who were absent without a valid excuse by laying them off for the same number of days that they had taken. New rules were promulgated which forbade punching in or out, except at the specified times. Finally, plans were made to stop using the sample room as the plant's "hospital." In sum, the whole indulgency pattern was subjected to a crippling attack, and workers' hostility toward Peele rapidly mounted.

Their resentment was, in part, expressed by making invidious comparisons between Peele and "Old Doug," the late manager.[2] The workers frequently and spontaneously recalled that Doug had hardly ever left his office to check up on things, but had used the phone to keep in touch, while Peele was always "standing over us." They emphasized that Doug had allowed them to take gypsum wall board freely, while Peele charged them for it. Thus Doug came to personify "leniency," while Peele was made to symbolize "strictness" or the violation of the indulgency pattern.

In part, workers conjured up the past, comparing Peele with "Old Doug," as an effort to legitimate the crumbling indulgency pattern and to justify their resistance to Peele's changes. If the elements of the indulgency pattern were suspect and non-legitimate, the

---

[2] We have elected to call this commonly observed pattern the "Rebecca Myth" and have discussed its manifestations more fully in *Patterns of Industrial Bureaucracy*.

myth of "Old Doug" became its guardian. The issue then need no longer be, "This is what we want," but could now be stated, "Old Doug did thus and so, and he was a good man." The development of this myth illustrates the workers' response to a "latent problem," and their use of informal rather than contractual solutions to meet Peele's violation of the indulgency pattern.

In the period following his succession, Peele also concentrated on improving board production, paying close attention to the installation of the new machinery. These machines, which consisted of a faster running conveyer, a better automatic knife, and a faster drying kiln, were being set up in the board building. Most of this installation work was handled by an outside contractor who hired his own men. The new machines were ready about the end of 1949.

The 1948 Cleavage

In the meanwhile, however, tensions in the changing plant had mounted. The men began to express fears that the new machines would mean an end to their overtime work and loss of their overtime pay. While they had not as yet suffered any economic loss, the workers began to demand higher hourly rates. In this way, they hoped to retain their former incomes even if their overtime should be eliminated.

By the spring of 1948 a sharp cleavage had developed between workers and the new management. At that time, and in accordance with the contract, the union gave management notice that it wished to re-open negotiations. The contract stipulated, however, that the only conditions permitting renegotiation were a "major change in the area rates of the industry or in the cost of living." Constrained as they were by these provisions, the union negotiating committee stuck grimly to the question of wages. They set aside all other grievances and advanced as their sole demand a request for a thirty cents an hour increase. The Company replied that, since there had been no changes in the area rates, only a two and one-half cents "cost of living" increase was warranted. Immediately, indignation at the Company's "insulting offer" ran high. While strike threats had been heard even before this, they now became more audible. The surface workers were somewhat less intransigent than the miners. "It's thirty cents or strike," growled the miners. "None of this haggling."

The men's argument for their thirty cents demand ran along the following lines: The new and faster machinery promised to eliminate their overtime pay. The Company replied that it did not intend to reduce the hours of work, at least until December, 1948. It also reminded workers that the contract provided that "if the Company reduces the work schedule from 48 hours per week to 40 hours, or less, this contract may be reopened."

The workers countered by saying that, if the Company could afford to spend $1,500,000 for new machinery, it could afford a raise. One of the emotional storm centers of the wage demand was the men's obvious anxiety about the consequences of the new machinery. This anxiety was intensified because the Company had never clarified what the results of the new machinery might be. Management had never sought to discuss any aspect of the machine installation with the men, and the men complained that they were being treated like "cogs." Moreover, the men invidiously compared management's two and one-half cents offer with the million and one-half dollars spent on the machines. This comparison undermined their self-esteem and made them feel less valuable to the Company than the new machinery.

Some of the men heatedly argued that the Company had made $12,500,000 in profits in the past eight years, and they wanted a share of it. They also reminded management that "the Company's board of directors had recently voted themselves a $250,000 bonus."

The workers stated, also, that the unskilled construction workers who were installing the new machines were being paid twice their rate "just for sitting on their asses." Management replied that construction work was seasonal, and that the construction men's *yearly* income was no more than the plant workers'. The workers jumped at this, saying, "Fine, we'll keep our present wage rate if the Company will grant us paid vacations equivalent to the construction workers' seasonal lay-offs."

Role of the Wage Issue

What appraisal may be made of the role of the "wage issue" in this situation? Was the conflict generated by it, or was it an expression of an already existent conflict rooted in other issues? Seen in the developing context of events, it seems clear that the wage issue here did not initiate the cleavage between workers and management but, on the contrary, the growing conflict precipitated the wage issue and, of course, was further reinforced by it.

One incident, which at least casts doubt on the importance of the overtime issue as a source of the cleavage, took place several weeks before wage negotiations began. One Friday, Peele told the board plant supervisor to inform certain men that they were to work on Sunday. After they were told this, the men expressed considerable unwillingness to come. When Sunday arrived, both workers and management were anxiously waiting to see what would happen. The men failed to come in. Deeply chagrined, Peele called Lakeport Monday morning and said that he was thinking of firing these men. Lakeport's answer was extremely cautious. Unwilling to contradict the plant manager openly on this comparatively minor question, it indicated that it was entirely up to him. He could fire the men, but on his responsibility alone. Peele changed his mind.

In this situation, the men had refused overtime work, even though it was on Sunday and would have earned them double their usual hourly rate. A typical explanation of their refusal was, "You just need some time off, and Sunday you have to have some time to go to church and sit with your family." This incident seems noteworthy for two reasons: (1) It suggests that the workers were not as intently anxious for overtime income as their later argument, during the negotiations, indicated. (2) If the workers had been well disposed or friendly toward management, they might have interpreted this offer of Sunday work as a favorable omen for their future overtime possibilities.

There were other signs, too, that the focus on the wage issue was a convenient vehicle for the expression of aggressions that had accumulated from other sources. These are evidenced in the union committee appraisal of its new regional director, Sundino. Comparing him with Garten, the man Sundino had recently replaced, one of the committee said: "Garten was good, but Sundino was *quicker*. When Binder (the Company's labor relations director) says something, Sundino jumps right in and before Binder can think, he's got him cornered." In other words, Sundino was liked not merely for what he was trying to get for the workers, but, also, because of the aggressive manner in which he sought to get it.

It is certainly not our intention to imply that the workers had no real interest in a wage raise, or that this was insignificant. So long as they live in a market economy, it is difficult to see how workers could fail to have such an interest; for in a market economy, very many of the things that workers, and others, seek can be secured only through cash transactions. Wages are therefore a key mechanism through which workers satisfy their wants and admit themselves to the social structure.

No one has put this matter more cogently than the conservative economist, Nassau Senior, when he commented that "wealth's possessor may satisfy at will his ambition, or vanity, or indolence, his public spirit or private benevolence; may multiply his means of obtaining bodily pleasure or of avoiding bodily discomfort, or the still more expensive amusements of the mind. Any one of these pursuits would exhaust the largest income; and as all men would engage in some of them, and many in all, the desire for wealth must be insatiable."[3] Needless to say, considerations of the sort Senior mentions played a role in the workers' wage demands. What is often neglected, and therefore deserves some emphasis, is that a wage demand also stems from other sources; here it was, among other things, a convenient way of expressing aggression derived from changes made in the plant's internal social organization, and especially from the attack on the indulgency pattern.

The Wage Issue and the Indulgency Pattern

Prior to the time that the new machinery was being installed, and even before the men began to strive actively for higher wages, many workers had felt that the plant's wages were too low. At that time, however, they had *not* made an issue of this because they felt that they were being well treated. As one worker expressed it then,

> "I like it here. They don't push you around. A man's got his work to do and they leave him alone. *You know that's one of the reasons they pay so low around here*. The Company knows that if they started getting tough around here, they would have to pay higher wages. The men would resent it and start asking for higher pay. *The pay is like a balance for the working conditions. It sort of balances things.*"

[3] Nassau W. Senior, *Industrial Efficiency and Social Economy*, Henry Holt and Co., New York, 1928, p. 65.

In other words, this worker was explicitly arguing that wages become a central issue when the indulgency pattern is violated and the Company "gets tough." This point is also made by another worker:

> "A while back the potash in the mix got tough on our hands. It caused all kinds of chapping and everybody began to get sores. The fellows in the shop got together—one of them had a sore on his hand the size of a quarter. He went to Peele. Peele looked at it, then shot into Johnson's (the board building superintendent) office. A few days later we had our regular safety meeting. I got up and spoke about our trouble. Johnson was there. He stood up quickly and said, 'Boys, there are gloves waiting in my office for you.' . . . *Certain things count a hell of a lot more than a backhanded nickel raise. There's a different feeling—you feel you're being listened to.*"

This comment also counterposes a wage raise (a "backhanded nickel") with "certain other things," particularly with demonstrated conformity on management's part to the workers' "protection" expectation, an element in the indulgency pattern.

The workers' emphasis on the wage issue was, in part, a response to management's violation of the indulgency pattern and, as such, contained elements of *retaliatory* aggression. The workers wanted to show management that "two can play at the game"; that they, too, could conduct their affairs in the impersonal, "business-like' manner that had been increasingly evident since Peele's succession.

To the extent that workers viewed the changing social situation in the plant as "increased strictness," and most did, their reaction was influenced by their notion of what was causing these changes. In large measure, workers perceived these changes as economically motivated. As one worker said bitterly, "They'll do anything to save a nickel." In other words, "strictness" was held to be due to the Company's effort to save money at the workers' expense. In such a setting, a wage demand became a punitive retaliation; it was an effort, as one worker put it, to "hit the Company where it hurt—in the pocketbook."

The workers' retailatory aggression was not, however, directed only against management's recent behavior. Their feelings about management were not based solely on a fear of *future* economic deprivation, nor even on dissatisfactions generated by Peele's violation of the indulgency pattern in the *current* situation. The happenings in the plant at that time were also being evaluated by the workers in terms of events which had occurred *long before*, but which were still well remembered.

In particular, many of the workers recalled the last depression and the callous attitude which they felt that management had expressed at that time. Typical of the comments made during the wage negotiations was the following:

> "You would come to work in the morning [during the 1930's] and the plant manager told you your wages were cut to 25 cents an hour. This stuff sticks in your craw; you don't forget that easily. The men were working then at 30 to 45 cents an hour for a 33 hour week. The plant manager put it down to 25 cents and said, 'If you want to work you can; if you don't, I can get plenty of men at that price'."

The depression of the thirties had been a gruelling, traumatic experience for the workers. During that period they had had to helplessly watch the complete dissolution of their indulgency expectancies under the pressure of economic exigencies. It had left the workers with a set of latent hostilities toward management that had been reactivated by the recent events. The workers' allusions to the last depression served both to justify and to intensify their aggressive behavior toward management.

If the strident emphasis on the wage issue was, in part, a product of the workers' resentment at changes in the internal organization of the plant, as well as reactivated depression hostilities, why was it that the workers did not express their "real" grievances? In other words, how did the hostilities engendered by changes in social relationships come to be displaced onto the wage issue?

Inhibition of the Non-Wage Grievances

(1) It has already been suggested that in the 1948 wage negotiations, contractual restraints played a part. In short, the contract itself, especially its wage renegotiation provisions, served as a lightning rod attracting diffuse aggressions which stemmed from various grievances. It provided a readily available channel into which other grievances could be poured, as well as cutting off opportunities for their direct expression.

(2) A second element constraining expression of the non-wage issues, which has already been referred to, was their lack of clear cut legitimacy. For example, workers were angry that no one had told them anything about the new machinery, and that management did not seem to be interested in their feelings concerning it. But they were not in the least certain that this was "their business"; they doubted that they had a right to complain about it. "Management feels the machines are none of our business," said a mill worker, "and maybe it's not." Doubting their legitimacy, workers could not readily make an issue of these complaints.

(3) Moreover, these non-wage grievances might be experienced in widely different ways by different workers. For example, absenteeism was one of the traditional ways in which miners demonstrated that "Down here we are our own boss" and they would, therefore, feel more strongly about the new restrictions against absenteeism than would surface men. Similarly, miners resented a "sneaky" foreman more than did surface workers. In consequence, such grievances could not readily provide a basis on which all workers might take concerted action. Unlike many other issues, however, a wage demand was one that most workers could support. As a board worker mentioned, when asked if the men would "stick together" in the event of a strike, "Sure . . . they all want to get more money."

(4) Other elements sidetracking the non-wage grievances involved the workers' relationships with people *outside* of the plant. Sympathy with complaints about the increasing "strictness" would require some familiarity with the workers' jobs and the plant's precedents. Since "outsiders" had less familiarity with the details of the workers' jobs, and with the ways in which the plant was changing, they could not easily comprehend and support the intense hostility engendered by Peele's actions.

(5) Moreover, the workers' wives, as well as the local storekeepers, would experience immediate deprivations in the event of a strike. Family cash reserves would have to be hoarded and expenditures made more guardedly. If a strike hinges on a wage issue, however, these "outsiders" might hope for some reward "in kind" for the losses immediately suffered. As a mechanic said, "The old woman had a fit when she heard there was strike talk, until I told her there'd be more money for a washing machine." Should there be no wage

demand, and the dispute solely concern inner-plant practices, no one but the workers themselves could hope to gain, even if a strike is won. For these reasons, the workers' outer-plant ties impel him to define his problem in terms of wages.

(6) Another factor exerting pressure in the same direction involved the situation in the local union leadership, particularly the new regional representative, Sundino. Being new, and also as the replacement for Garten whom many workers had liked, Sundino was in a position where, as he said, he had to "prove himself." As he saw it, this meant that he had to "get something for the men." But being new, Sundino also lacked familiarity with the recent plant changes and did not feel secure in using these as his lever. A militant demand for a wage increase was, therefore, about the only issue he felt secure in raising.

(7) Furthermore, profits and wages, unlike the more subtle changes in the plant, were readily observable indices of plant conditions; they could be watched and evaluated by national union officers far from the scene. In short, a local wage dispute seems to be more readily managed by a distant headquarters. Beyond this, however, the national headquarters could also provide more tangible assistance to a local union, giving it, as it did to the Oscar Center workers, statistical data about Company earnings, the cost of the new machinery, and information about the bonuses for the board of directors. "Since Sundino came in as union organizer," remarked a board worker, "we get all these statistics about the Company's profits."

(8) To the Company, wages were an understandable issue of relatively high legitimacy; it was an issue which was not conceived of as threatening managerial prerogatives. The Company was forced by competitive pressures to place considerable stress on wages, and especially, on "comparative area rates of the industry."

While reviewing a list of union demands that had been submitted to the Company at an earlier time, we noticed that they had each been translated into a specific number, which was their expected dollar cost to the Company. "The boys upstairs can figure it out to the fifth decimal point," explained a main office executive with amused satisfaction.

Not all union demands, however, can be translated with equal precision and ease into their dollars and cents implications. The pecuniary implications of a *wage* demand can be arrived at simply;

but how are the cost consequences of, say, eliminating punishments for absenteeism to be reliably calculated? To the extent that a wage issue has *calculable* consequences to management, it will be easier to bargain with a Company on this than on other questions. This is another element in the situation directing attention toward wage questions and away from others.

In the light of these considerations it is easier to undersand how the wage issue comes to overshadow other grievances and why, frequently, complaints stemming from changes in plant practices are channelled into a demand for more money.

The Outcome of the 1948 Negotiations

Shortly after the men rejected the Company's two and one-half cents offer, the union took a strike vote, thereby complying with the legal regulations for the conduct of a strike. At this tense time a state mediator was called in, and, at the next negotiation meeting, the Company increased its offer to ten cents an hour. This increase did not, however, result only from the increased imminence of a strike or the efforts of the mediator. It was connected also with developments in a nearby plant, run by the Company's chief competitor, where the workers had just been granted a ten cents an hour increase.

During the luncheon adjournment of this meeting, Tenzman and Crackery, two members of the union committee, went on a tour of the plant. Shortly after the meeting reconvened, another of the union's committee, Izzaboss, a welder in the mine, heard his name called by someone outside the window. Claiming that he thought it was his "driver," the man with whom he customarily rode home from work, he went to the window and "saw all the men lined up outside."

Seeking to impress management with their determination, the men from the board plant had stopped work. The union disclaimed responsibility for this walkout. Nevertheless, there was a prevalent belief, among workers and management alike, that Crackery had given word for the walkout when he made his luncheon tour of the plant. Whether or not this is actually correct, it is consonant with the volatile and excitable behavior of the surfacemen's leadership.

Byta, the union's president, took no active leadership role, despite his formal position as head of the local. Here he initiated a pattern that was to be repeated in the 1950 wildcat strike. Leadership fell into the hands of the negotiating committee, two of whom, Izzaboss and Nate, were miners, while two, Crackery and Tenzman, were surface workers.

As distinct from the explosiveness of the surface leaders, those from the mine were more even-tempered. As the dispute wore on, the miners' leaders assumed a studied, slightly self-conscious dignity. After the walkout, surface men and miners treated their leaders quite differently. The surface workers evinced considerable hostility toward Crackery, apparently relieving themselves of their subsequent guilt feelings, by blaming him for what they later held to be an unnecessary walkout. Shortly after the negotiations were settled, Crackery bid for and took a position as a truck driver, which kept him away from the plant and the critical workers.

In contrast, Izzaboss' status among the miners was enhanced. His behavior became that of a leader confident of the approval and support of his followers. His new role, bringing with it greater self-esteem, is indicated in a report by one of the research team:

> "[The day after the walkout] Izzaboss deliberately kept us standing a few minutes while he triple-tested a joint he had just welded. This was unlike his customary approach which was characterized by immediate greeting. As soon as our conversation started, the other men in the shop gathered around and I immediately realized that Izzaboss had acquired greater status. . . . The customary exchange of friendly obscenities which usually fell somewhere around the opening of any conversation with him was skipped, and he began by asking what we wanted to know from him."

Shortly after the walkout, the Company increased its offer, partly at the prompting of the state mediator, to twelve and one-half cents an hour, which the workers finally accepted. From this time forward, however, the plant was tense with minor crises centering on the new machinery; grievances among both miners and surface workers more frequently flared in overt shows of hostility.

The Second Succession

For almost two years the plant remained in this state of tension. In January of 1950, an event occurred that jolted the uneasy equilibrium: Peele, the successor, was succeeded. A new plant manager,

Landman, was brought in and he, in turn, made a number of "strategic replacements" among the middle management. Peele was demoted to a job as supervisor in the maintenance department. Three other supervisors, each of whom had worked for the Company for twenty years or more, were demoted.

SUMMARY OF THE SEQUENCE OF SUCCESSIONS

Office	Before First Succession	First Succession	Second Succession
Plant Manager	Old Doug	Peele	Landman
Safety and Personnel Manager	Day	Digger	Gudeguy
Board Plant Superintendent	Johnson	Johnson	Watson
Office Manager	Cook	Cook	Digger

Johnson, head of the board building, was given a foreman's job and was replaced by Watson, who had worked in another of the Company's plants. Cook, the office manager, was demoted to a clerk in his own office and was replaced by Digger. An "outside" man, Gudeguy, took over Digger's former job as plant personnel and safety manager. Finally, the head of the warehouse was demoted to a foreman there, and a foreman in a different department took over his job.

Three months after these changes occurred, the workers walked out and the wildcat strike was on.

Chapter Three

THE ZONES OF DISTURBANCE

SHORTLY BEFORE NOON on a pleasant April day in 1950, the men at the Oscar Center Plant walked off their jobs. They stayed out for ten days. While men at other Company plants throughout the country had from time to time walked out, this was the first "real" strike that the Oscar Center Plant had ever known.

Without formal notice, without a strike vote or planning, and in the midst of routine production, the men in the board plant determined to quit. From there the strike spread to other divisions, to the mill, to the machine shop, and down into the mine. By noon, the machines' clatter had halted completely. With the exception of the office workers and supervisory staff, who remained to "clean up," the production workers had gone home to lunch or had retired to a nearby tavern to talk about the strike over a cold beer.

No pickets were posted. A few men remained to tell the next shift that a strike was in progress. After this was done the plant's gates were deserted; apart from supervisors' and office workers' cars, the parking lot was emptied. Thus the strike resembled but little the conventional newspaper accounts of modern labor-management conflict. Aside from its unplanned, unheralded, and undemonstrative quality, the strike may have also seemed strange to readers of the evening paper in nearby Lakeport who noticed that the workers had made *no wage demands*. Other grievances had at last found a tongue.

Members of the research team, interestingly enough, did not find the strike a "surprise." Neither did we consider the omission of a wage demand so remarkable. For more than a year and a half we had looked upon the strike as "inevitable"; and this prescience was no monopoly of the researchers. For both management and the workers also found little about the strike that was unanticipated. When the labor relations director of the company was asked whether he knew the strike was coming, he replied: "Yes. We've been struggling against time since last January." The union secretary, Bill Sodlen, confirmed this: "The powder keg was set," he said, "They were filling it for *three years*, even better. Nobody along the line has taken the interest to find out, to help in a matter that could have been stopped long ago. They were forewarned at the time they changed in the sample room (i.e., replaced Day with Digger). Warned the time I went to Lakeport. They must have realized long ago about our reaction and the state which we were in."

An interesting problem which must at some point be considered in analyzing the strike is this: How was it that forewarned did not mean forearmed? How did it happen that an *anticipated event*, one which men on both sides of the dispute foresaw and did not desire, nevertheless came about?

Just Before the Strike

For some time before the Oscar Center strike, the Company's plant in Big City had been out on strike. Unable to get production out of the Big City plant, main office management rerouted some of the more urgent orders to Oscar Center. One such order was particularly noted at the plant. This was a shipment for export to South America and, since this was unusual at Oscar Center, it attracted the men's attention.

Having heard of this, the Big City local contacted Bill Kayo, the Gas, Coke and Chemical Workers' regional director, and Tony Sundino's immediate superior. Big City asked Kayo to stop shipment of the export order and, if necessary, to picket the Oscar Center plant. On the other side, however, the Company's Lakeport office "asked Bill" to get that one important order out. They told him that, unless they could ship it, they would be compelled to turn the order over to one of their competitors. Kayo agreed to go along with the Company's main office. He did so because the Big City plant was not organized by the Gas, Coke, and Chemical Workers; in fact, it was a part of John L. Lewis' District 50, with whom the president of the national Gas, Coke and Chemical Workers had long been feuding. The president of the local, Byta, also agreed to get the export shipment out, and management felt that both he and Kayo were being very cooperative. Nevertheless, the plant workers intensely resented working on this order and were restrained from going out on strike at that time only with some difficulty.

Alongside of this problem other difficulties, those involving the new machinery, were simultaneously coming to a head. The Company had recently assigned one of its production specialists, Jack Spiedman, to the job of improving the "change-over" operations at the take-off end of the board machine. Spiedman was a "practical" engineer who went from plant to plant straightening out technical difficulties. He had been assigned to cut down the time it took take-off men to change from handling one type of board to another. Formerly, the change-over had taken about twenty minutes; but Spiedman had told the supervisors, who told their workers, that he intended to cut this time down to 2 to 4 minutes.

Spiedman had been at this assignment for several weeks prior to the outbreak of the strike. About a week before the strike the men had complained that Spiedman was using supervisors to assist on the take-off change. They claimed that this violated the contract clause, which prohibited supervisors from working except under emergency conditions. The union committee told the Company that foremen and supervisors would be permitted to work only when they were instructing workers in the new changeover techniques, and they could have only thirty days for an instruction period. Main office management agreed to this, feeling that Byta had to be given some concessions so that he could keep his men in hand.

The union executive committee instructed Tenzman, now chief steward, to keep watch on the take-off operations and see that their demands were met. This was done to satisfy the men at the take-off end, who were especially anxious that a union representative be present. The take-off workers were angry because the machines they used were old and inefficient, unlike the other machinery newly installed in the board plant. They complained that it was too difficult to wheel the changeover machines into position, since they weighed more than 500 pounds and needed to be pushed over a rutted cement floor.

On the morning of the strike Spiedman had announced that they would try for a four-minute changeover. Standing astride one of the machines, Spiedman saw Tenzman among a group of foremen who were all watching the preparations. Spiedman climbed down and contacted Tenzman's foreman, Hismeade. "Listen Hismeade," he told him, "there's one of your men by the machine and we don't want him there." Grasping Tenzman by the arm, Hismeade led him away.

A few minutes later Spiedman and Tenzman met at the "coke" machine. (The two of them had had a long-standing personal quarrel, springing from a dispute in which Tenzman had told the engineer that another war would be a good thing. Spiedman, who had lost a brother in the war, had demanded to know how Tenzman had gotten out of being in the army. He ended this argument by calling Tenzman a "yellow bastard.") Upon seeing Tenzman at the coke machine, Spiedman snapped, "What the hell's the matter with you, Charlie?" "You know what's the matter," Tenzman snapped back. "Why I've got half a mind to hit you, you yellow bastard," Spiedman said. Apparently at that moment Tenzman made up his mind. He announced that work would stop in two hours, thus giving management a chance to cut off the board machine in advance, and prepare for an orderly shutdown. The strike was on.

The Symptoms Considered

The above description is primarily a statement of symptoms which reflect a larger and more complex social situation. However, if these symptoms are taken as a point of *departure*, on the assumption that they are connected with less visible components of the situation, they lead back to an understanding of some of the more fundamental conditions underlying the strike.

A. The Export Order

If taken at its face value, the workers' hostility to the export order, from the strike-bound Big City plant, was a curious response. This was certainly not a sentiment born of *class*-conscious solidarity with fellow workers in distress. For it would be difficult to imagine these Republican, farm-rooted workers adopting the sentiments of militant class-conscious solidarity. Nor can their resentment be explained as a result of loyalty to their *union*. As pointed out, the union leadership did not want to strike on such an issue for their own political reasons; moreover, they were able to sympathize with the Company's desire to get this order out. It is true, of course, that "labor unity" is a permissible definition of such a situation in trade union circles, and one with which the workers were familiar as a slogan. As such it provided a readily available language for justifying and expressing existent hostilities.

There was no indication, however, that the workers objected to the export order because they felt morally obliged to aid the Big City workers. There is reason, though, to believe that some of their motives may have been expedient; that is, if they supported the striking Big City workers they could hope for reciprocal help when their own time came. Nevertheless this does not explain the show of affect, the strong feeling and strike threats, against the export order. In fact it leaves the analysis precisely where it started. For if the workers did act expediently, extending help in calculated anticipation that they were opening an account for future withdrawals, then it is still necessary to explain why they were *ready* to strike.

Actually the workers had almost forgotten this export incident by the time they had gone on strike. While on strike none of them made the slightest reference to it, and in no way indicated that this was something they were striking against. The significance of the export incident instead appears to be along different lines.

The mere presence of the export order was a constant *reminder* that another of the Company's plants was out on strike. The export order had to be shipped differently and, since it was being produced for the Big City plant, distinctive kinds of "stickers" indicating compliance with specific Big City standards, had to be pasted on every piece of board. Noticing these unusual stickers go by, the board workers were continually prompted to talk about the Big City strike and its implications.

One obvious implication of this strike was the Company's weakness at the moment, a weakness which suggested that it was a comparatively safe time for the Oscar Center workers to express aggression. It announced, in effect, that this was a tactically appropriate moment for a strike. But another implication of the Big City strike was even more important to the Oscar Center workers; namely, that the Big City strike could be used to legitimate their grievances. "We're not the only ones who feel this way," explained a worker, "The boys in Big City didn't go on strike for nothing, you know." The export order's presence in the plant was thus taken as a confirmation of their own hostile judgments of the Company.

In brief, the export order played an important role in bringing about the strike at that specific time. As a symptom, however, it suggests the presence of freefloating aggression ready to be discharged by a small stimulus; but it gives no indication of the *sources* of the underlying cleavage and aggression.

B. The Case of the Cursing Supervisor

In contrast with workers' later disregard of the export order incident, the men evinced widespread and continuing interest in Spiedman's role, and were later inclined to blame him for the strike. Most workers saw him as a major precipitant of the strike and, after it had begun, demanded that the Company move him out of the plant. Two aspects of his behavior on the day of the strike left an enduring impression. The first was that he had sworn at Tenzman; the second, that he had "overstepped his bounds."

So widespread was the first complaint that even a local gas station owner gave his preliminary explanation of the strike in these terms:

> "From what I can get at, it's this new *travelling* superintendent they have. He's what you call a travelling superintendent or supervisor. Seems as though he's been using strong language with the men. Told off a committeeman, called him a yellow bastard. He has no respect for the men."

Like other human behavior, swearing assumes its meaning in a context, as the burlesqued Westerner's threat, "Smile, when you say that, podner," implies. An interview with Crackery makes this point explicitly:

> *(I heard a bit about swearing. Do the men swear much?)*
>
> "You don't find it much on top, either in the plant or in the mill. *In the mines, there's more.* But the foreman don't cuss at the men."
>
> *(You mean the foremen on the surface never swear at the men?)*
>
> "Well, I suppose they do. But there's a difference in how they swear at a man."
>
> *(A difference?)*
>
> "Sure, if you're kidding around and swear it's O.K. But if you're serious and swear, you're liable to get your nose punched in."
>
> *(How do you know a man's serious?)*
>
> "Oh, through his conversation. He tells you if he's serious

or kidding. If he calls you a son of a pup while he has a serious face, if he's peeved and then swears. Like when he gives you an order and then swears. You know he's not kidding. That's a horse of a different color. Personality makes a difference. With a good guy, you know he's a straight shooter. If a guy is ugly *he swears to agitate you. To show that he's better than you."*

Crackery's comments suggest, then, that to the workers swearing is permissible only in the context of a friendly, informal relationship, that is, from a "good guy." When it occurs in a conflict-saturated setting it is resented. It is then interpreted as an overt sign of aggression, particularly disturbing to the surfacemen who ordinarily stress the renunciation of open aggression. For these men swearing was also often experienced as an expression of "disrespect," that is, as an attack on their status, because they believed that it was typical of the "groundhogs" or "low caste" miners.

In sum, the workers' resentment at Spiedman's swearing was symptomatic of the deterioration of friendly, informal relations between themselves and sections of their supervisors. Spiedman's isolation from the workers epitomized the widening cleavage between the supervisors and men. Since he was a *travelling* supervisor, who moved from plant to plant, he had no chance to integrate himself into a stable pattern of informal relations. Consequently, he did not have available a fund of "good will," or personal friendliness, which he could draw upon to implement his efforts. In this respect he was sharply contrasted with the demoted supervisors whom the men had known intimately for many years. One worker put it this way:

> "They (the demoted supervisors) never *had* to talk to the men like that. Spiedman called one of our men a yellow bastard. Told him it was none of his Goddamned business if he wanted to speed up the machine. The men couldn't keep up with the machine and this Spiedman wanted it to go faster, and this new supervisor, Watson, is no good either. The old supervisors didn't tell them what to do."

Moreover, since Spiedman could be expected to leave the plant shortly after completing his assignment he was not, despite his authority, an individual whom it would "pay to suckhole." There is a peculiar dilemma evident in his position: By virtue of his insulation from the plant's informal organization, his drive for efficiency was unfettered by informal ties and obligations. On the other hand, however, this very same insulation prevented his efforts from easy innovation. For he was unaware of the hornet's nest that his work was stirring up, and he had no informal resources that could ease the tensions he aroused.

Not only did Spiedman antagonize the workers, but he also threatened and angered some of their supervisors. The supervisors and foremen resented his assumption of authority and his efforts to modify practices with which they were long familiar. They interpreted his very entrance into the plant as an implied criticism of their own procedures. Hence supervisors as well as workers resented Spiedman. As the union secretary, Sodlen, summed it up, "He was against the willingness of the men." His "bullying" behavior is not to be seen, therefore, solely as a personal idiosyncrasy. It was brought about, at least in part, by his isolated position in the plant's social organization, by his separation from both informal and formal mechanisms of persuasion and control. He was therefore constrained to use punitive and aggressive techniques.

Another aspect of Spiedman's behavior was especially criticized by Sodlen, as well as other workers: namely, what they called his "overstepping of the bounds." This, too, was a criticism directed against other supervisors as well, and particularly against Digger. Sodlen had specifically objected to Spiedman's calling upon Tenzman's supervisor to remove him from the scene of the take-off work.

> "Where does Spiedman get off to tell the foreman what to tell his men. He overstepped his bounds. An engineer is there to read the blueprints and to help with the technical aid. But he can't have anything to do with the men. I asked Hismeade [Tenzman's foreman], "Has he the right to ask foremen where his men are?' "

Sodlen and others concerned about supervisors' "overstepping of the bounds" were, in effect, raising a question about the legitimacy of a supervisor's authority in a given area. This grievance did not criticize the plant's authority system as a whole but was, instead, a complaint about an individual. Replace this individual with one who will know his limits, notably the established plant practices, ran the implication, and peace may be restored. Along similar lines, some workers explicitly disavowed any desire to change the plant's formal arrangements and indicated, instead, a desire to restore things as they had been. When asked what the men expected to gain from the strike, one mill worker stated, "They want to leave it like it was before." In part, then, some workers defined the strike as an effort to restore the older pattern of relationships with management.

This complaint reveals that in the course of "overstepping," deeply internalized values have been outraged. The very language of the criticism and the affect accompanying it express moral indignation. One can overstep the "bounds of *decency*," but not the "bounds of efficiency." The language is appropriate only when morally toned expectations have been breeched. At some point attention must therefore be turned to the nature of these violated expectations.

Taking issue about foremen who "overstep their bounds" may also constitute a demand to know "who is boss here," as well as what it is that they have authority over. Commenting on the relations between Peele and Digger, Sodlen expresses what had come to be, by the time of the second succession, a widespread grievance against them:

> "Digger was to take over safety conditions when he came. When you went to him you were by-passed. . . . Everything was by-passed. The fellows didn't know if Digger or Peele was the supervisor [i.e., Plant Manager]. Digger did the work. He'd promise the fellows a lot of stuff. Later he'd lie about it. He wasn't honest."

Uncertainty about who possesses authority creates tensions for workers because it then becomes difficult for them to know who is obligated to them, or to which person they in turn are obligated. The vague location of authority need not be quite so disturbing, however, if workers' relations with their superiors involved a friendly confidence born of informal ties. When suspicion replaces an expectation that each will do his duty, when supervisors come to be viewed as persons who break their promises, as dishonest and sneaky, then it becomes necessary to "pin them down" and carefully specify their sphere of authority. In other words, when workers demand to know "who is in charge here," and that "the boss should be the boss," they are giving vent to previously developed conflict-attitudes; they want to know, in effect, whom they can blame.

C. "BROKEN PROMISES"

In defining their injuries as "broken promises," workers sought to disqualify *local* management as an acceptable group with whom a solution could be reached. As Sodlen noted:

> "The men on the board machine wanted to shut down right away. We tried to talk to them. They said you guys are gonna take *more promises* from the Company, more lies. So we told the Company, *we wanted to talk to somebody greater*, that we didn't know the new men very well. The guys said they wouldn't talk with them. *We wanted higher-up* authorities."

In effect, the charge that local management broke their promises provided justification for going over their heads to executives in the main office. Since such a measure was commonly viewed as a last resort, workers had to have "solid" grounds to excuse this violation of precedent. The violation of a "promise" also symbolized the fracturing of informal group ties. "We could *believe* the old foremen," said one mill worker. "We knew them. But these new fellows, that's another matter." In short, the breakdown in "trust" between workers and management seems to have been connected with the second succession and the strategic replacements which followed it.

Furthermore, to state that local management was derelict because it "broke promises" is to imply that they had already accepted as legitimate certain claims made by the workers. Claims which management has itself acknowledged, by virtue of the promises made, are thus all the more a justification for retaliation if later ignored or rejected.

It was not, moreover, a *single* promise which the Company was held to have broken but *many* promises. "The union committee found that there was a pile-up on grievances," said Crackery. What is important is the cumulative aspect, the "pile-up on grievances," the history of unfilled promises:

> "There were a lot of grievances that the Company wasn't handling. . . . The Company wouldn't pay much attention to the grievances. They wouldn't fulfill their promises."

In short, the grievances were experienced as long-nourished and deep-going. This raises the problem of why was it that the existent grievance machinery proved inadequate, thereby allowing the workers' aggression to mount to a point where it poured over into action? It is a problem that will need to be considered at a later point.

D. The Machines Went Faster

Among the revealing grievances voiced by workers were their complaints about the increased speed of the new board machines. Hostility toward Spiedman was in part symptomatic of this complaint, since it was his special job to speed up production. Typical of this explanation of the strike were Sodlen's comments:

> "They want to make a faster change-over [referring to Spiedman's work at the take-off end]. *It means that the right man has to be at the right spot at the right minute.*"

"The new machines made a lot of difference," remarked Crackery. "They step up the machine and the guys aren't used to it. It irks them to think that the machine is going faster."

Of course, only one section of the surface operations was *directly* affected by introduction of the new machines. The mine, maintenance, and the mill had had no faster operating machinery recently installed. Nevertheless, other operations in the plant were indirectly affected when the board machines set a faster pace. For example, the maintenance men had to be on their toes to a greater degree since any breakdown would have more costly consequences, both in bad board produced and in the amount of good board that could not be produced while the machine was being repaired. Similarly, greater amounts of gyp had to be calcined in the mill and dug out of the mines.

But all sections of the plant were not *equally* affected. Comparatively little change was required to handle the increased need for stucco in the mill. Moreover, the miners gave no evidence of minding the demand for more gyp. In the main, the supply of gypsum ore was determined by the richness of the vein that was being worked. Hence the new board machines did not require equally great increases in "work effort" from all. In a later chapter we shall want to examine just what it was about the new machines that angered the workers.

E. Foremen Working

The introduction of the new machinery did increase the likelihood that foremen would take some part in the actual work process, and provided more occasions for workers' complaints about "working foremen." But the sheer fact of a foreman working does not, by itself, elicit a hostile response from workers. More decisive however are the collateral behaviors of the foreman; i.e., whether he uses the occasion to increase his supervision and exert closer control over the workers. The men discriminate between certain kinds of foremen, whom they do not mind working, and others to whom they take exception. As one of the miners states:

> "I'm a pump man and if the foreman wants to come around and help me, it's O.K. If he says, let's get that tap off so I can check it, then if he wants to take the wrench and do it, why not? Or if he hands me a piece of pipe or a wrench while we're doing something together, that's all right. But most of the foremen aren't like that. Take H———, he'll come around and tell you what to do. As long as he's going to butt in I'd tell him to do it himself. When I want my foreman or if something is wrong he'll help out. . . . I know he's doing it to help me. *H——— is just doing it so he can tell you what to do. So he can be important and above the men.*"

Hostility to foremen working is, then, a complaint about "close supervision"; it arises when foremen use the occasion to increase their control over workers. The increasing prevalence of the "working foremen" grievance, therefore, seems indicative of the men's increased hostility to closer supervision.

The workers did not mind a "working foreman," moreover, if they were closely identified or friendly with him. Under these circumstances the foreman's working was likely to be seen as a form of democratic behavior. It proved the foreman did not "act superior." It was not uncommon, in the earlier phases of our study, when the new machines had not yet been installed and when workers were closer to their foremen, to hear workers *commend* the plant precisely because foremen *did* work. For example, a wet-end man commented then:

> "Out here we get along well. Everybody's reasonable. Foremen, you see, are what you call working foremen, they work right along with the men. . . ."

Our analysis, however, sharply contrasts with the explanations which the workers themselves gave in accounting for their hostility to working foremen. Their stated reasons were rationalistic and were couched in the language of trade union solidarity: "It takes away another man's job if a foreman works," they said. Actually, though, few if any foremen worked with anything like the regularity that would be required if they were to "do another man out of a job." Our own analysis suggests, instead, that the men were angry about working foremen not because this hurt *others* who *might* be employed by the plant, but because it adversely affected *themselves*—those *already* employed in the plant. For reasons needing clarification, the foremen had begun to tighten their supervisory control over workers, in a setting in which informal relations between the two groups had deteriorated. Resenting this, the workers used the formal rules of the contract, which provided that foremen could not work except under emergency conditions, as a convenient tool with which to strike back.

Chapter Four

MANAGEMENT'S AND WORKERS' IMAGES OF THE STRIKE

THE GRIEVANCES mentioned in the last chapter were not all equally stressed by the conflicting parties and, sometimes, the "same" grievance meant different things to different people. Here we wish to examine these grievances in terms of *who* held them, noting the divergent emphasis and meaning which management and workers gave to the issues involved. If the way in which the conflicting parties saw the strike is known, it may help to explain how they later sought to cope with it. For the solutions they adopted derived in part from the ways in which they looked upon the strike.

MANAGEMENT'S IMAGE OF THE STRIKE

Our intention is not to outline management's entire definition of the strike but, principally, to focus on its *distinctive* emphasis. In particular, top management's assessment of the situation is vital, for they were the managerial echelon which could make the crucial decisions. While they could not resolve the strike in disregard of lower management's sentiments, they had the final voice.

In larger measure than the workers, top management at the Lakeport office conceived of the strike as the product of a calculated stratagem by the workers. Unlike the workers, they felt that the "export order" figured importantly in the events that brought the strike about. One of the main office executives began his account of the strike with a detailed statement of the union's and workers' reaction to the export order and emphasized, particularly, the tactical advantages which workers may have thought they possessed in view of the strike at the Big City plant.

Management also tended to conceive of the strike as a *struggle for control* of the plant. It was not quite a pure struggle for power, not entirely a power conflict, but it is rather close to it and may become even more clearly so in the future, their conception suggested: "The workers don't look at the strike in the light that 'we've got the strength'," mused a main office executive. "Yet they have a strong desire to run the plants."

The power conflict view of the strike is important because it implies that workers' grievances are in the nature of an ideology, masking their underlying intentions. Behind each specific complaint, the power politics definition implies, there is a hint of a fundamental challenge to management's status. In this context the problem readily becomes, not the adjudication of each grievance or the modification of the circumstances which elicit it, but rather the need to reaffirm "who is boss here!" A staff supervisor, one of the engineers in the plant, voices this sentiment:

> "The supervisors are kind of kicked around by the union. If there's a grievance they get it too. They [the workers] got a chip on their shoulders. They think they are more important than the Company. All this is going to be changed. They'll know the foreman is the foreman."

There are at least two important functions served by defining a dispute in terms of its power connotations:

(1) This view allows management to obviate questions concerning the *validity* of the grievances. In bypassing the ethical facet of the conflict, it thus allows management to do whatever is necessary in order to "handle" or control the situation. In this way, the issue is trimmed to a problem in "social technology"; the question then becomes one of choosing *efficient* means of control. For if management senses a fundamental challenge, the emergence of a pure power struggle for dominance, it feels justified in choosing *any* solution that will enable it to win.

(2) Moreover, definition of a conflict in power terms is in itself an "ideological" mechanism, peculiarly useful to those who require some escape from a moral crisis. If a disputant doubts the legitimacy of his own side's position, his ability to defend himself before a public, or before his own conscience, is undermined. He may sidestep this difficulty, however, by implying that the ethical

dimensions of the conflict are really peripheral; that is, he may claim that they are merely window-dressing to conceal the real issue, the pure power conflict.

One section of management, that centering around the labor relations department, had hoped that efforts at a strike settlement would be postponed. They were somewhat sorry that negotiations had begun immediately after the strike started. They had hoped, they said, that the situation would have an opportunity to "cool off" before talks began. After the negotiations began, they looked upon them as an opportunity for "catharsis," providing the worker with a chance to "blow off steam and clear the air." Here, too, as in the power struggle definition of the strike, there was a tendency to view the manifest content of the workers' grievances as somewhat secondary; "getting it off their chests" was held to be the vital thing, rather than resolving the specific grievances about which the affect centered. Emotions and feelings were conceived of as dangerous, and were seen as inhibiting a "reasonable" settlement.

In effect, a section of top management had tended to conceive of themselves as therapists. In this role, they took account of the workers' unconscious and irrational emotions, which were held to be at the root of the difficulty. To suggest that a section of management tended to use the therapist's role as a model is no mere literary figure. Along these lines, and as partial cause and effect, was the Company's support of a superior "human relations" program. This employed a series of motion picture strips, which analyzed group tensions from a psychoanalytical viewpoint, in terms of the unconscious needs of individuals, and which were discussed with foremen and workers throughout the Company.

The foregoing indicates then, that a section of top management viewed the strike as a combination of impersonal, cold-blooded calculation of the tactical opportunities, and an irrational emotional outburst.[1] This double-barrelled conception of the strike may seem to be

---

[1] The "power conflict" and "emotional outburst" views are two widespread conceptions which management groups have of labor-management relations, though not the only ones. Another common view, which is not openly displayed in crisis situations, is a conception of the situation as a "game." Thus labor relations directors will often feel and express genuine excitement about their work, and enjoyment in their relations with union representatives. They will em-

contradictory, but this need not be actually so. The production department seemed to be more heavily committed to the "power struggle" view, while the personnel department was more inclined to the "emotional outburst" conception. Thus these somewhat mutually exclusive views were not held with equal emphasis by all sections of management.

Nor were they applied with equal emphasis to all groups of workers. There was a tendency for management to speak of the workers' *leaders* as if they were motivated by rational and tactical considerations, while the *rank and file* of the workers were usually held to be motivated by emotional forces.

These two views of the strike do, however, have at least one thing in common. They both bypass the question of the legitimacy of the strike. For questions of "right" and "wrong" are as irrelevant in a power conflict for survival as they are in the relations between a therapist and patient.

Management's avoidance of the value aspects of the question

---

phasize often that their relations with union functionaries are devoid of feelings of hostility. The game viewpoint comes out most clearly when, for example, a labor relations director comments that each side knows the routine that the other will follow in the negotiations. One labor relations director once remarked to me that the union representative and himself joked about changing sides in a forthcoming negotiations session, and suggested that either one of them could probably do well at the other's job. This seems to reflect the "objectivity" of the expert so disturbing to his client. Labor relations can take on "game" characteristics when each party is aware of the structural constraints that the other is laboring under. For example, when the union leader knows that the company labor relations man operates in terms of limits set by higher management and cannot transcend them, and when the labor relations man is aware that the union leader *must* bring home some settlement with which he can pacify his own rank and file. If each tacitly expresses awareness of the other's limitations, and signals his intention not to violate them, then a game is being played in which union leaders and company labor relations directors may develop no little camaraderie. In sum, the game framework is one of stable equilibrium between the two players, not merely because each is satisfying the expectations of the other, but because each is helping the other to satisfy the expectations of some *third* party.

clearly suggests that they were uneasy about the moral propriety of their own arguments and behavior. Indeed, main office personnel explicitly indicated this. After discussing the causes of the strike at length with one executive, he finally said that, in his opinion, the "key" thing was that "the fellows just didn't have confidence in the company." "Why didn't they have confidence in the company?" he was asked. He replied:

> "*It would be amazing if they had confidence.* On January 15th, we changed from Peele to Landman [the second successor to plant manager]. Johnson and Cook were also demoted and *they both had their watches. If a man works twenty years for the Company he gets a gold watch.* From then in he is referred to as 'having his watch.' Cook became a clerk in his own office [from office manager]. He has his watch too. These changes *justify* the 'no confidence'."

In other words, this executive was very disturbed by the demotion of men who had long-standing seniority in the plant. Of course, this executive, like others, believed that impersonal and objective criteria of demotion and promotion, a man's "efficiency," should determine his career in the Company. On the other hand, however, most executives also believed that "seniority" should be given consideration in personnel relations.

Management's adherence to seniority was attested to by their custom of issuing gold watches for twenty years' service. It was also acknowledged in the Company's labor relations manual:

> Length of service increases are considered by the Company on the basis of the years of satisfactory service rendered by an employee. . . . For the first two or three years of service in a position such increases are synonymous with merit increases. However, the Company recognizes that an employee continues to become more valuable with years of service, even though increased value is difficult to measure accurately. *Also, the Company feels that an employee with years of service in a position should receive some monetary appreciation for faithfulness.* [Emphasis supplied—a.w.g.]

This affirmation of seniority, in an inter-office memorandum, is indicative of the sentiments of its writers (who were main office executives) and the anticipated sentiments of the managerial corps to whom they were writing. Yet the strategic replacements among foremen had injured precisely those supervisors with the longest seniority.

Notice, too, that the manual indicates that long-standing seniority is taken as an earnest of *"faithfulness"* or loyalty to the Company. In effect, management's drive for efficiency had led them to demote men whom they, themselves, looked upon as unusually loyal to the Company. Management could not help but feel that, at least in some measure, its own behavior was improper; and for this reason they felt the men justified in withholding "confidence" from the Company.

This tension between "seniority" and "efficiency" reflects a basic managerial dilemma. In order to preserve the security of the enterprise, management wants men who are *both* loyal (and seniority is commonly taken as an index of this) and efficient. Since the loyalty and efficiency of its working force, and especially of its supervisory cadre, are fundamental managerial interests, the choice of one at the expense of the other is bound to place management in a threatening and unsettling quandary.

Since the Production Department was mainly responsible for the costs and level of production, it felt compelled to choose efficiency rather than seniority. The production executives were focussing on the *technological* consequences of their decision since these most directly affected their own department's position. The *social* consequences, the possibilities of conflict that might result from violating the group's seniority expectations, comprised a danger of which they *were aware* but felt they had to risk. The labor relations department, on the other hand, anticipating these conflicts and knowing that it would be *their* responsibility to cope with them, tended to oppose the production department's decision. As one member of labor relations said, "Under proper leadership, I think that they [the demoted supervisors] could have functioned all right." Being the more powerful department, the decision of the production executives prevailed.

There was at least one other reason, peculiar to this Company perhaps, why the main office executives paid more than "lip service" to "seniority" and were genuinely disturbed at its violation. This involved the Company's distinctive competitive position.

The Company's major competitor is the "Monotuff" Gypsum Company, whose president is widely reputed to be a bitter "antilabor" man. Monotuff is viewed by many of the Lakeport executive staff as the brute antithesis of what they would like the General

Gypsum Company to be. Many of General's executives had once worked for Monotuff and were rankled at the latter's methods of treating their employees, managerial or otherwise. As the director of production explained:

> "I spent eleven years with Monotuff Gypsum. Believe me our democratic spirit didn't prevail there. A good many of us came from Monotuff. They treat people as machines and tools. They haven't any understanding of human relations. We treat people as human beings."

General's interest in "sound human relations" constituted a continuing polemic against Monotuff, and was another arena in which a nation-wide competition could be pursued. For this reason, too, the demotion of the old supervisors upset the members of the executive staff.

The Workers' Image of the Strike

The great majority of workers viewed their strike as a justified and legitimate action. Workers usually defined the strike in ethical terms, holding it to be morally justified. As many of them said, "We're out to get our rights." The strike was not interpreted by them, as management was inclined to define it, in the amoral concepts of power. Their hostility toward the "swearing" supervisor, and against supervisors who overstepped their bounds, expressed *moral* indignation.

Far from presenting their action as a deliberately calculated stratagem, the ordinary worker emphasized its *spontaneity*. They spoke of the plant as a "powderkeg" which had "blown up" in the unpredictable manner of a natural eruption, rather than in accordance with the purposive planning of men. Even some of the top union leadership were surprised at the spontaneity and solidarity evinced by the workers. "This walkout was a spontaneous reaction," Kayo observed,

> "They just walked off the job and went home. They didn't bother to picket or anything. They just stayed home. I've never seen such complete action. The guys came to the union officers and said they were going to walk out, and that's all."

Each of the grievances that workers actually emphasized as justification for their strike had two facets. In each grievance two different outlooks were operative; one was oriented to established plant practices and was morally indignant at the violation of these custom-grounded expectations. This may be called the "traditionalist" outlook. The other, or "marketing outlook," was oriented to more formal expectations and was hostile at the infringement of the contractual agreement. Different workers gave the "same" verbalized grievance a somewhat different "twist" depending on their outlook.

Those oriented to the established practices interpreted the "swearing supervisor" grievance as an expression of unbecoming "coldness" and "unfriendliness"; those having a formal outlook saw the same grievance as a rejection of "inequality"; to them a swearing supervisor was one who made unjustified claims to superiority. From the perspective of those concerned with established practices, supervisors who "overstepped their bounds" were violating traditional plant practices which they believed should govern the relations between workers and foremen. In the view of those who were contractually oriented, this same grievance meant that supervisors were wrong in assuming powers that had not been explicitly and *formally* granted to them. This group would not have been so affronted at the violation of established plant practices, if the foremen's behavior had been officially sanctioned.

When those concerned with the defense of established plant practices spoke of "broken promises," they seemed to mean that the supervisors had violated a "trust." To the contractually oriented group of workers, "broken promises" meant that supers had broken commitments explicitly acknowledged and contractually binding. When those oriented to the established practices complained that the "machines went faster," it largely appeared to be a grievance to the effect that management no longer had any limits to what they wanted. In the formal-contractual outlook, this grievance meant that workers were being forced to work harder without a *quid pro quo,* without more money. Finally, when those concerned with traditional practices complained about "foremen working" they meant that supervisors no longer left you alone and did not trust you to do your work properly. To those contractually oriented, this grievance meant that working foremen were "taking another man's job away."[2]

---

[2] The "export order" has been omitted because our protocols do not reveal that the men were actually motivated by this grievance.

Each of these two orientations was not only emphasized by different workers, but was occasionally voiced by the same worker. Sodlen, for example, after complaining about the effects of the speed-up at the take-off reveals both viewpoints:

> "Other plants with machines like ours make the change in two to four minutes. Can't blame them [management] for wanting to cut down from twenty to two minutes. But the take-off has used the same machinery for twenty years, the bundler and all."

Thus the union secretary sympathized with both the Company and the workers; he was ambivalent about the Company's speed-up and about the workers' demands; in the end he finds the Company at fault only because it was technologically backward and inefficient.

A similar ambivalence was found among some of the small businessmen in the community, one of whom explained the demotion of the old foremen as follows:

> "After all, they're supposed to keep him on because he's been with them for a long time. But a big corporation isn't that way. If they can find someone better to do the job, they put him there. You know, a new broom sweeps clean. Take these old foremen. They were demoted and put to work like the men they used to supervise. The fellows feel stinkin' about this. But after fourteen or fifteen years a guy gets in a rut. So you have to do something about it. After all, they gave them a chance to get on a paying basis. . . . After a guy gets to know you he'll ——— you every time."

These comments indicate that the obligatory force of seniority expectations was acknowledged. But so, too, is that of the expectation of efficiency, for as he says, the plant must be kept on a "paying basis." And as he adds elsewhere, "The plant is *right* in making them work more and better if they're losing money."

In consequence of this split in outlook, two different definitions of the strike were developed by workers. Stated in purified and extreme form, those who were custom-rooted sought a *restoration* of the past. They wanted a return to previously existent worker-supervisor relationships in which management's expectations would not be constantly changing. They sought no change in the authority *system* as such but instead, tended to focus their aggression on an *individual*, Spiedman. Their strike thus conforms to the classic pattern of a traditionalist rebellion which, in Max Weber's words, "is directed against the person of the chief or of a member of his staff [i.e., the travelling engineer]. The accusation is that he has failed to observe the traditional limits of this authority [i.e., overstepped the bounds]."[3] In brief, they sought the road back.

For these "traditionalists," the strike was an expression of resistance against the prolonged and continual violation of their old beliefs. In another respect, it was a demand for increasing the predictability with which their established privileges would be satisfied; that is, for a cessation of "broken promises." In greatest measure, their hostility was directed against changes which had affected the *informal* organization of the plant's social system, for it was in this sphere that their customary rights resided.

On the other hand, the "market-oriented" definition of the strike, extremely stated again, sought no return to the past but, instead, looked forward to *changes* in the *formal* organization of the plant as a remedy for their grievances. They dwelled upon the failure of certain formal mechanisms, especially the breakdown of the grievance machinery, in bringing the strike about. In addition, they wanted their trade union to participate in determining the speed of production. "This is fundamental," said Bill Kayo, "Management [in other companies] does this all the time." They sought, also, a solution to the problem of "working foremen" by having top management issue more clear-cut directives to foremen ordering stricter conformance to the contract. These "market men" did not seek to transform the informally established and traditional practices into formal contractual terms. Instead they sought formal recognition of *new* rights and obligations, such as control over speed norms.

For the "market men," the strike expressed an effort to formally locate managerial responsibility ("Who is boss here?") and expressed resistance to inadequate contractual conformance. In general, they emphasized the pecuniary implications of the workers' grievances; thus the "speed-up" was perceived by them as more work for the same money. They also accented the *contractual* roots of the strike.

---

[3] Talcott Parsons and L. Henderson, *Max Weber: The Theory of Social and Economic Organization,* p. 342.

Speaking of the "radical" group on the union grievance committee, Sodlen commented that they were able to make trouble, " 'cause of the way the *contract is written.* You can find trouble every day if you want to." In his view the strike was occasioned by a "misunderstanding of the contract."

In many ways, the "market men" among the union leaders looked upon the strike in a manner very similar to the labor relations executives among top management. For example, these union leaders believed the strike to have come about because some of the men "lost their heads" and gave vent to irrational feelings. Like top management, too, the "market men" among the union leaders also viewed their relationship with management as reflecting a power struggle. They felt that sections of management were deliberately acting in a way that threatened the prerogatives and position of the union. Sodlen, for example, said that plant management had once offered the boilermen a larger wage increase than they had been willing to offer the union negotiating committee. In fact, he added, they finally gave the boilermen a larger increase than the one the union committee had recommended. "They were trying to break us," declared Sodlen, "They were trying to show the guys that they could work without the committee."

If the traditionalists sought a return to a relationship governed by "trust," then the "market men" desired a situation in which trust did not matter; they wanted their prerogatives safeguarded by legal guarantee. If the traditionalists wanted to be able to return to the "fold," the "market men" wanted to be "taken into the business." If the traditionalists wanted workers and management to be "friends," the "market men" wanted them to be "partners." In sum, the traditionalists wanted a return to the old indulgency pattern, while the "market men" were willing to set aside the informal privileges of the indulgency pattern in exchange for new, formally acknowledged union powers.

Though both of these outlooks were to be found throughout the strike, there seems little doubt that the traditionalists' definition of the strike dominated in the beginning. Suggesting this is the unplanned and "spontaneous" character of the walkout, the initial focussing of grievances on the behavior of an individual supervisor, the absence of a well formulated set of union demands, the deep feeling against the demotion of the old supervisors. Also indicating that the "market men" did not initially lead the strike was the fact that Byta and Sodlen, who were generally regarded as the "conservative" union leaders, half stepped aside, and were half shouldered aside, by Izzaboss who took over the leadership of the wildcat strike, as he had taken over the leadership of the "quickie" in 1948.

Chapter Five

CAUSES OF THE STRIKE

IN THE FOLLOWING PAGES, we will attempt to explain how this strike occurred. In doing so, however, no effort will be made to deal with "all" the strike causes, as this is never possible. Instead, what we will do is to trace the role of a variety of factors, such as the "succession," "strategic replacements," and "indulgency pattern," showing how they contributed to the outbreak of the strike, and illustrating their utility for the analysis of organizational dynamics.

WHAT IS A STRIKE?

Before proceeding, however, one major ambiguity must be resolved. However simple the term "strike" may seem at first, closer inspection reveals that it is not without difficulty for scientific usage. A "strike" is a social phenomenon of enormous complexity which, in its totality, is never susceptible to complete description, let alone complete explanation.

Some might characterize a strike as a "refusal by the employees of an establishment to work"; others might speak of a strike as a "concerted withdrawal from work by a part or all of the employees." "A typical juridical definition of a strike is, 'a combination whereby the body of workmen refuse to carry on work unless their demands are met by their employer'." It is obvious that a strike can be defined in somewhat different ways, each of which can be valid and useful for different purposes.[1] There is one element, however, which is com-

[1] The quotations in the preceding paragraph are from E. T. Hiller, *The Strike,* University of Chicago Press, Chicago, 1928, pp. 12-13. This is one of the very few studies of strikes made from a sociological viewpoint. Hiller's study is typically American in its concern with the practical techniques which each side uses to maintain social control over its own forces when a strike takes place. As Hiller

mon to the above, as to most definitions of a strike; this is that the technological consequences are placed foremost. It is spoken of as a cessation of "work," that is, as a breakdown in the flow of materials within the factory and of the flow of commodities to the community.

A second and closely related specification of a strike is to conceive of it as a *refusal to obey* those socially prescribed as authorities in that situation, that is, management. By defining a strike as a "refusal to obey," we deliberately focus on matters of specific sociological interest, the breakdown in the flow of *consent*; we address ourselves to the disruption of a social system, particularly in its authority relations.

A third relevant aspect of a "strike" is that it constituted, at least in this case, an open expression of aggression. It is useful to conceive of a strike in this way since "aggression" is a factor in a complex body of socio-psychological theory which can be helpful in the analysis of data. We appreciate, of course, that some strikes *seem* to take place without aggressive expressions. We say "seem," because there really is very little evidence on this point. In any event, we elect to focus on the strike as an aggressive form of behavior because it would appear that this is its more socially significant form. If strikes took place without aggression, it is doubtful if anyone's applecart would be upset. In short, the aggression laden strike is likely to have a greater impact on and significance for the surrounding social system than one devoid of aggression.

Having set down what we mean by the term "strike," we are now in a position to start our analysis. There are three factors which the examination of the strike symptoms repeatedly brought to attention, the technological innovations, the succession, and the strategic replacements among middle management. Let us begin to trace

---

says, "Adequate causes for striking are necessarily assumed, but the problem as to how and why action in a particular situation becomes collective is equally important." Ibid., p. 24. Our work will complement Hiller's in that, while he takes the "collective" character of the strike as the central problem for analysis, it will be treated as a "given" by us; conversely, while he takes the strike's causes as "given," they will be problematical for us. Another way of saying this is that Hiller was largely concerned about the relationship between worker and worker, while we are primarily concerned with the relationship between workers and management.

their connection with the strike by examining, in greater detail, the technological changes.

The Technological Changes

Here there seem to be two critical questions: (1) Did the technological innovations as such arouse the workers' aggression, or was this the result of the way in which these changes were *administered* and of the *social* changes which accompanied them? (2) What was the specific nature of the administrative and social changes accompanying the technological innovations?

The introduction of new board machinery, it must be emphasized, did not merely make for a *faster* operation but had other significant consequences as well; two of these also swelled the workers' hostility. One was the *unstable* speed of the machines; the other was the change which was brought about in the workers' *supervisory situation.*

To consider the first point: Since the machines were new, their optimal board output had not yet been definitely determined. During one week, for example, the machine might run board at 135 feet per minute, the next week at 140 feet per minute, and so on. Joe Cook, brother of the demoted office manager, emphasized that there had once been a *limit* on the Company's production expectations:

> "When I first started working for General Gypsum around 1926, we had our production quota and sometimes we could finish at twelve and quit for the rest of the day."

There seems to be no production limit during the period when a new machine's potentialities are first being explored. For some reason, the absence of a limit to management's production expectations was, by and of itself, experienced as threatening and wrong by many workers. At the beginning of 1950, Sundino had therefore written to Peele asking him to state just how fast the machines would finally run, explaining that the men were concerned about the question. Peele replied, "The nature of our product is such that we cannot forecast expected speed. It must be understood the formulas are continually being changed and the effect it might have on speed is unpredictable."

While production norms were being experimented with, management was also likely to stay *nearer* to the scene of operations, and to make more insistent demands upon the workers for "alertness." It meant, also, that main office executives, or *higher* echelon supervisors who were *unfamiliar* to the workers, were on the scene more frequently than usual. The Spiedman case epitomized both of these tendencies. Thus one of the often unnoticed by-products of technological change is a social change in the supervisory situation.

Under these pressures workers were unable to make easy, habitual responses in their work behavior. As a warehouse worker remarked: "The men are not used to the speed of the machine and it will be a headache until they are. They'll like it after they get used to it and it's *automatic*." The men were made "nervous" by the presence of unfamiliar "brass," by the foremen who engage in closer supervision and by their increased demands for alertness.

In fine, it was not the speed-up as such, or even the increased physical energy required, which alone can account for the way in which the machinery affected workers' attitudes. Consideration must also be given the effects of *unstable* speed norms, of *closer supervision,* and the *modification of work practices* which simultaneously occurred. All of these pressures compelled the workers to pay closer attention to their jobs, to *commit* themselves to their work, to psychologically "participate" rather than merely to be "active." As a knifeman put it with a revealing slip of the tongue: "They want you to be more incensed [sic!] about your job, to take a better interest in it."

These considerations about the newness of the machinery were clearly important for the board plant, where the strike broke out. The new machinery did, however, also affect other workers, especially to the extent that it provoked a *generalized* drive toward increased efficiency. With the introduction of the new machinery, a mill worker explained, "the supervisors were told to *bear down* by the higher-ups." Pressure was placed on the plant manager to use the new machines efficiently and to guarantee that the *entire* plant, which was operated as a single budgetary unit, would begin to pay for them.

Purchase of new machinery, especially as it entailed a large outlay, was a managerial decision to which considerable attention was given. It became a moment of "stock-taking," both literally and figuratively. It was a time for careful assessment of the level and effectiveness of operations throughout the whole plant. In one respect, then, purchase of new machinery created pressures for the entire plant, bringing many established patterns of behavior and expectation up for reexamination.

The purchase of the new machines also reorganized management's attention. It *increased* management's concern about technical problems and organization, about production norms and quotas. In so doing, however, it *distracted* managerial attention from problems in the sphere of plant social organization. Bill Kayo's explanation of the strike makes this point quite clearly:

> "The Company installed a lot of new machinery . . . and they didn't know how much it would produce. Well, they ran into trouble and *they completely ignored the tensions among the workers* which developed . . . They were interested only in getting more production."

Thus even though work equipment in many sections of the plant had not changed, and while most workers did not have to "work harder," nonetheless almost all of them experienced anxiety-provoking demands for alertness and were subjected to closer supervision.

One factor influencing workers' attitudes toward the new machinery requires further comment; this involves their relationship with the supervisory staff. The remaining, older foremen's hostile attitude toward the new machinery was noticed by the workers. They observed that "even the foremen didn't like it," and did not like Spiedman who personified the process.

Johnson, later demoted as superintendent of the board building, had been a focal point of supervisory resistance toward the new machine, and he had continually resisted efforts to raise its speed. His specific reasons for doing so are interesting: The faster the machine went, the greater the wastage of board in event of a breakdown. If the machine was *not* working at its optimum speed when a breakdown occurred, then there was *less* wasted board. When that happened Johnson would *temporarily* increase the machine's speed and make up the wasted board. In this way no one would be the wiser; Peele would never know there had been a breakdown and Johnson would escape criticism. If, however, the machine worked at full speed continually, there was no way of making up wastage without calling it to management's attention. Partly for this reason,

Johnson had resisted the effort to increase the board machine's speed, and the older foremen under him had shared his feelings. In short, increased machine speeds had wiped out the "safety margin" in Johnson's relations with his superiors, making it next to impossible for him to conceal any failure to come up to their expectations.

Of general significance, however, were the older foremen's negative attitudes toward the machines which served to *justify* the workers' own hostility. In rejecting the new machinery the workers were at one with the older foremen. Those workers closely identified with the older foremen would thus have another reason for resisting the technological changes; knowing that some of the foremen agreed with them, these workers felt freer to *openly* express their gripes about the machinery. This, then, is another way in which workers' relations with their supervisors influenced their attitudes toward the machines.

The workers also knew that some *men* determined what the machines would do. *Who* these men were, and how the workers *felt* toward them, significantly affected their attitudes toward the speed-up. For example, one worker was asked:

> *(What if the speed-up would have come with the older foremen here?)*
>
> "Well, they know the men better." he answered. "He knows the work they have to go through. He's done it himself. I don't know, but *they probably would not have resented it so much."*

Clearly, *attitudes toward the new machines were affected by the second succession and the wave of strategic replacements accompanying it.* For if the men were more friendly with the remaining old supervisors, as they were apt to be, their resentment toward the machines was reinforced by the old foremen's critical attitudes. If they were hostile to the successor and the new supervisors this, too, increased their resentment of the machinery and its concomitants. The machinery did not generate hostility simply because it made some of the men work harder in a physical sense. Attitudes toward the machinery were also affected by the changing social relations between supervisors and workers while, in turn, these relations were affected by attitudes toward the new machinery.

In sum, the workers' hostility was not aroused by the technological changes alone, but also resulted from the fact that they were subjected to "closer supervision" during the experimental phase of the new machines' introduction. The complaints about "working foremen," who just try to show that "they are boss," and the hostility directed toward Spiedman's bullying behavior, suggest that management was operating in a status-emphasizing, deference-demanding manner. This violated an important element in the indulgency pattern, the workers' expectation that they were "there just to do a job."

Looking more closely at Spiedman's behavior, it may be seen that it was, in microcosm, a reflection of the larger tendency to make the changes in a dominating, authority-stressing way. Spiedman was very devoted to the Company; he had worked his way up from the bottom and had been with it for a long while. He was not a college trained engineer but had, instead, acquired special familiarity with the mechanics of gypsum machinery during his career with the Company; it was for this reason that he was known as a "practical" engineer.

Some years ago, Spiedman's wife had died, leaving him to raise their son alone. He was a lonely man, and his job, which required that he travel from one Company plant to another, intensified his loneliness. He badly wanted acceptance from top management, but being away from the main office, and being unrooted in any one of the plants, Spiedman could rarely get the recognition he sought. When drunk, he would complain self-pityingly, "Appreciation and recognition are more important than money."

When he entered a plant to do a job, Spiedman experienced his isolation from the rest of the supervisors and workers acutely, and conceived of it as a rejection, which it often was. To this he responded by "showing them up." Spiedman was proud of his ability to work hard, and bragged that he could spend 36 hours without a rest while working on some problem. He liked to take "cat naps" for a couple of hours and would return to his work when no one else was around. Working secretively, and never letting other people in on his ideas and plans, he would suddenly "spring" it on them. After finishing his job, he would braggingly call attention to his achievement and imply that the others must have been stupid not to have seen the solution.

Spiedman is thus an excellent example of the dynamics of sadistic rationalism, where intelligence and work become instruments of aggressive domination, where they are used for status and ego inflation, rather than for the sake of accomplishing the task itself. This, of course, outraged the workers who were more "task-oriented," and who expected that authority would be used mainly to facilitate work, rather than having work used to enhance authority.

It remains to be added that main office management knew how Spiedman worked and related to people; while somewhat wary of his "bull in the china shop" approach, the Lakeport executives were primarily concerned with his technological skill, rather than his social ineptitude. Since they tended to define "success" technologically, rather than socially, the main office thought of Spiedman as a "good man with certain eccentricities."

Succession and Strategic Replacements

The above discussion has already indicated that the second succession and its wave of strategic replacements increased the workers' hostility to the new machinery, directly adding to the aggression which had been mounting since the "first" succession. Workers' and other community members' comments about the role of succession and strategic replacements are somewhat paradoxical. They rarely began their explanation of the strike with reference to these events but they rarely ended without mentioning them; once mentioned, however, they were commented on with considerable feeling.

One of the ministers of a community church began his explanation of the strike by referring to "the adjustments which have to be made when they handled different size boards" at the take-off. In talking on, however, he added, "There hasn't been very good feeling in the plant *since the demotion of the old men.*" He finally concluded that the "adjustments" at the take-off end "seemed to be the final straw"; in other words, they were a precipitant rather than a basic determinant of the strike.

Sodlen, in fact, indicated that the beginnings of the strike were even to be found as far back as Peele's succession, and could not be understood solely as a result of Landman's succession:

> "*It's been starting the last three years.* We had a change in supervision three years ago—the personnel manager and the superintendent."

The workers' hostility toward Landman, the new plant manager, and toward his new supervisors, was directed at the manner in which they had been appointed to their new offices, and to the way in which they behaved once appointed. Landman, in particular, was castigated as an efficiency-minded manager who was solely concerned about the *main office's* evaluation of him, but who had no regard for what the *workers* thought of him. As one board man remarked:

> "The only word I know for him, like the men call him, is just a plain p - - - k. He is a guy that wants the men to work on their job and stick a broom up their ass and sweep the floor at the same time. He's looking out for himself. He's the kind of a guy who'd stick a knife in you when he could. Wants to make a name for himself."
>
> *(In what way?)*
>
> "Well, he wants to make things look good . . . get production up. He doesn't give a damn for any of the men. The men resent the whole set up. They don't like anything about it."

The men did not dislike Landman simply because he was new and a successor; they also disliked him because of the way in which he *behaved*. Of course, the way in which he performed his role, especially his sensitivity about satisfying the main office's efficiency expectations, is a reaction common to successors. In the main, the workers focussed their aggression on Landman's efficiency-minded behavior and experienced it as demeaning and status-degrading.[2] Comments

---

[2] My psychiatric friends suggest that certain psychoanalytical speculations may prove fruitful here. They call attention to the language of the workers' complaints and especially their "earthy" imagery. Freudians, they say, might be tempted to suggest that, on a deeper personality level, the behavior of the new manager aroused homosexual fears. Notice he is a "penis" and would "stick a broom [sic!] up their ass," or "knife you." The terms characterizing management's behavior are classical in their symbolic significance. The knife may be interpreted both as a penis surrogate as well as a castrational implement; and if the knife is to eunuchize the workers, the broom—a penis symbol with homosexual designs—is, in a double sense, available to force them into "women's work." Brought to focus on the problem, the psychoanalytical hunch might be that, for some men, the strike was motivated, on a very deep and unconscious level, by a desire to ward off a homosexual attack. At any rate, psychoanalysts have advanced more "outrageous" hypotheses than these. For

about the new head of the board building also made a similar complaint: *the workers felt Watson's behavior* to be a status threat, saying he "acts superior," "treats you like a 'nigger'," and behaves like a "slave driver." In the words of a take-off man:

> "Take this new guy, he's *a Southerner* who just came up from the South . . . He's a slave driver and a pusher. Used to talking to a lot of 'niggers' so he acts superior. Probably knows what he's doing, but he doesn't treat the men right."

Workers were hostile to the new administrative staff, then, not merely because they were heightening the plant's efficiency, and demanding more work, *but also because of the status-threatening and deference-demanding ways in which this was done.* The workers felt that the new management was acting "superior" and believed that they were being degraded. The changes were disrupting the plant, in short, because the new management was behaving in a way that violated the workers' indulgency expectations that they were there "just to work."

EFFECTS ON THE INFORMAL SOCIAL ORGANIZATION

One of the most important results of the strategic replacements, following both successions, was that it accelerated the breakdown of friendships between workers and supervisors, so that the latter came to be regarded as "outsiders." For example, the new board plant superintendent was quickly identified as a "Southerner," as someone clearly devoid of the symbols of in-group membership.

The manner in which a foreman performed his job also affected his community relations with the men. The men did not want to be friendly with the new foremen outside of the plant, because the latter's behavior within the plant was felt to be improper. One miner was asked, "Do you tip a beer once in a while with the foremen?" and replied,

---

our own part, we feel that it is adequate to indicate here that the strike was motivated by the attack on statuses which were deeply internalized in the worker's ego and which had been identified with fundamental conceptions of himself, especially his manhood, and by the resulting violation of the worker's technologically oriented conception of his factory role.

"Once in a while we do. We did more often with the older foremen. Some of the newer foremen aren't too friendly and the men don't want them to be either."

(Why is this?)

"Well, a fellow like ———, for example, isn't too much fun outside of work. Too many men are sore at him for things he does in the plant."

The foremen's behavior toward the men, and the consequent feelings which the men developed about the foremen, were incompatible with friendly ties. Workers especially resented the new foremen's reliance upon punishment and coercive supervision. As a mill worker remarked:

"Guys like [two of the demoted supervisors] . . . never *had* to talk to the men like that. They knocked down a few of the foremen and this new board superintendent is no good either. Now the men don't want to cooperate with the supervisors. They feel he *makes slaves of them*. The men like the demoted supervisors. *They didn't tell them what to do. They didn't crack the whip over them.*"

The workers' relations with the old foremen were based on a friendly confidence; conversely, the increased use of punishment and close supervision by the new foremen was occasioned by their poor informal connection with the workers. Formerly, the personal ties between workers and foremen had enabled, in fact, had bound the old foremen to "trust" the workers. Now the strategic replacements had brought in new supervisors who did not know the men well and, who, therefore, did not trust them as much. As a mechanic said:

"They don't have confidence in the men 'cause they don't know them; naturally they keep *close watch* on them. They think we aren't willing to do a real day's work."

Acting on the widespread belief that informal relations between those who are not formal equals impairs efficiency, most of the new supervisors were afraid to get "too close" to the workers. As the men felt it, "they didn't give a damn for any of the men." However, the new safety and personnel manager, Gudeguy, did not feel this way and did not resist integration into the workers' friendship groups;

as a result, he was quickly accepted by the workers and was not the object of hostile attitudes. When one worker expressed a liking for Gudeguy, he was asked:

> *(How come that Gudeguy's new and well-liked?)*
>
> "He was broken in by the Company over here. They broke him in here. He's a swell egg. He'll talk to you. Kid along . . . he has a way about him. He's likeable, not afraid to admit when he's wrong, and not afraid to speak up when he wants to. We can tease him. He smokes a real big pipe and we tease him about it. It's a joke with the men. He's a good Joe."

Having previously been trained at the plant, the "new" personnel man was not entirely new. He had had an opportunity to establish personal ties with several plant workers during his original training period, before the drive for efficiency was in full swing. As a not-so-new-comer, his comparative familiarity with the plant and greater security in it allowed him to accept informal ties to a greater extent than other strategic replacements. Since he had been in the plant for a training period before Landman's succession, the workers did not identify him with the new order of things. In the main, however, the net effect of the strategic replacements was to reduce the degree of informal solidarity between workers and supervisors. And this made the workers feel all the more "left out of things." With the decline in friendship between workers and supervisors, the formal authority system became the basic social cement. The formal status distinctions between worker and supervisor were no longer blurred, and instead differences in power and authority became overt and visible. An indication of this was the increased tendency of the newer supervisors to demand deference from the workers, that is, to "*show* who's boss."

Where, as in the case of Gudeguy, a new supervisor did not "pull his rank" on them, the men accepted him. In the main, however, because the strategic replacements were new and somewhat insecure, because they had defined friendship with workers as threatening, it was hard for them to relate informally with the workers. They therefore had to fall back upon their formal status to get things done, and demanded obedience mainly on the impersonal grounds that "they were boss," thus violating the work-centered expectations of the indulgency pattern.

The Decline in Work Motivation

One of the responses which workers made to these violations of their expectations was "withdrawal"; that is, they tended to remove themselves either from emotional participation or even physical participation in the plant. Discussing the changes in machinery, for example, one worker mentioned, "Twelve men quit for every six hired because they don't like working where changes are continually occurring."

Withdrawal took a different form in different contexts. In the sphere of informal contacts, workers withdrew from friendships with foremen. As a mechanic said, "I wouldn't even give the time of day to a foreman like that." In the formal status system, withdrawal expressed itself by withholding support from the formal ends of the organization production. As a miner remarked, "The way to get along with these new guys [foremen] is to do as little as you can get away with, but let them see you working when they're around."

It seems conceivable, though, that the developments which threatened the workers might have been met by intensified efforts to gain acceptance from management, rather than by withdrawal. The men might have felt that by "working harder," management would become more friendly and relax its close supervision. But the workers had defined the older foremen, who had been demoted, as paragons of conformity. They had been conceived of as particularly loyal to the Company. For example, it was frequently commented by the workers that these men had *not* quit the Company, during the war, in order to take better paying jobs in defense plants. When these men were demoted, therefore, many workers began to feel that "it didn't pay to be a good guy in this plant." In part for this reason, then, withdrawal defenses were first utilized by workers when their expectations were frustrated.

Paradoxically, strategic replacements, one of the devices management employed to raise plant productivity, resulted in a decline in the willingness of the workers to produce. The drive for efficiency had the unanticipated consequence of impairing one important source of efficiency, the motivation to work. The men themselves clearly recognized that they would not work as hard for the *new* foremen as they did for the older ones. In the words of the demoted office manager, Bill Cook:

> "I've known [one of the demoted foremen] for over twenty years, and he is one of the finest bosses that a man had. *The men will do a day's work for him and over.* He is sincere, honest, and a good worker."

Asked how the men worked under the new foremen, another worker replied:

> "Well, they don't give them the *cooperation* they gave the other guys. *The other foremen would never of had this trouble.*"

Obedience and Work

It is clear, of course, that the line between motivation to work, and motivation to obey, is a thin one. Workers themselves usually made no such explicit distinction, and included both working and obeying under the heading of "cooperation." Since "work" is a managerial expectation, and since it takes place under the direction of supervisors and foremen, "working" occurred within the framework of authority relationships. The degeneration of motives for work, therefore, also involved an unwillingness to obey. When, for example, a worker was *told* to "get a hustle on," if he did not do so, he was disobeying as well as not producing properly.

The close connection between motivations to work and to obey may be seen more clearly if a distinction is made between two types of low work motivation, or as labor economists call it, "restriction of output." In the first case, the withdrawal is a passive one and the worker feels "apathetic" about his job. For example, one worker said, "I do what I have to do, and no more; after all you can't get anywhere anyhow." On the other hand, there is a second type of withdrawal containing covert aggressive feelings. This is a deliberate withholding of work effort as a way of retaliating against a superior; it is akin to Veblen's notion of a "*conscientious* withdrawal of efficiency." In this vein, a mill worker declares, "The more that s.o.b. pushes me, the longer I'm going to take; even if it kills me."

Both types of low work motivation are incompatible with high motivations for obedience; for a willingness to obey would constrain the individual to produce. The second type, the deliberate withdrawal of efficiency, has even more direct implications for obedience, being only a thinly disguised expression of hostility towards superiors. In short, there is no clear-cut separation between low motivations to work and to obey; each tends to spill over into the other and each tends to be induced by similar pressures.

The Legitimacy of Authority

As Max Weber has stressed, the chance that an authority will be given obedience is dependent in part upon whether his subordinates view his authority as legitimate. If the subordinate believes that the authority is a "rightful" occupant of his office, then obedience is no longer given only as a matter of expedience, in hope of some reward or fear of punisment, but becomes a morally binding obligation. In this case, to use psychoanalytic terms, obedience is motivated by "super-ego" or conscience promptings, while disobedience would be inhibited by internalized mechanisms such as guilt, and not merely by fear.

Legitimacy was denied to the new management on a variety of grounds. It was denied, first, because the *old* foremen's removal was considered illegitimate. The formula announcing a succession is, "The King is *dead*, long live the King." Workers did not accept the removal of the old supervisors; believing them to have been invalidly deposed and that the Company was behaving ungratefully to workers of proven loyalty, they would not accept their successors as legitimate.

They charged that the new foremen were not really more efficient than those whom they had replaced, describing the former as men who "only pretend to be busy." They asserted that the replacements had not attained their new positions because of their competence, but through the use of "underhanded methods." They also refused to accept the new supervisors because they "showed no consideration for the men," and treated them as "slaves" rather than as "human beings."

In effect, the workers were saying that a legitimate supervisor is one who conforms to the indulgency pattern and does not engage in close supervision; he is task-oriented rather than status-oriented. Diverging from these expectations, the new management refused to set aside status differences, refused to joke and be "kidded with," or to engage in bull sessions with the workers.

Finally, the workers also expected that the "boss should be the boss," that there should be someone in the plant who could give them a definite "yes" or "no" to their demands. In part, this is a criterion of legitimacy more appropriate to the days of small independent enterprises, in which the manager is also owner. Here, of course, the manager was not; he was subordinate to other managers in the Lakeport office whose approval he had to maintain. While this is a pattern to be discussed more fully in a later chapter, it may be mentioned here that the *succession* of two managers within a brief time span meant that the man in charge of an unfamiliar plant was likely to act cautiously and with an indecision that workers derided as "unmanly." For these reasons then, the new management was not conceived of as legitimate, and workers' motivations to give it consent and obedience were further undermined.

Tensions in the Mine

We have observed, so far, that the technological changes, the succession, and the strategic replacements aroused aggression and lowered workers' motivation to work and to obey. They did so, in part, because they generated close supervision which violated the workers' indulgency pattern. The situation in the mine, thus far neglected, is interesting because it reveals the disruptive consequences of close supervision which was not initiated by recent supervisory or technological changes.

About three years before the wildcat strike, and shortly after Peele's succession, a new mine foreman, Ferdinand, had been sent over from Peele's former plant. Like other foremen in the mine, Ferdinand was now subordinate to "Old Bull," the mine superintendent. Years ago, however, when they had both worked at this other plant, their positions had been reversed; then Old Bull had been a foreman in the mine, while Ferdinand had been the mine superintendent.

Upon coming to the Oscar Center plant, Ferdinand began to compete with Old Bull for control of the mine, and openly expressed his intention of taking over the latter's job. Unfortunately for this aspiration, Ferdinand was not accepted by the miners. Unlike Old Bull, Ferdinand was a status-conscious supervisor, much disposed, as the miners put it, "to throw his weight around," and ordering the men about in an impersonal and authoritarian way. For example, he would decide that a given mining room was safe to work, and would insist that the miners work there despite their objections. This evoked considerable criticism of Ferdinand and, on one occasion, provoked a short walkout among some miners.

Ferdinand became the object of widespread "kidding" which intimated that he was sexually impotent. The miners' "evidence" for this was that, though he had been married for many years and was a Catholic, he nonetheless had no children. Ferdinand found the kidding difficult to take, for it was a sensitive point in a group of men such as the miners who stress their masculinity; as a result, he was only very loosely integrated in the formal structure of the mine and, unlike Old Bull, was unable to get things done without "pulling his rank."

Old Bull and Ferdinand personified the conflict between the indulgency pattern and the forces which were undermining it; the miners' rejection of Ferdinand, and their alliance with Old Bull, reflected their preference. There was no evidence that the miners disliked Ferdinand because he wanted to make them work harder; in fact, there never was any question about the vigor and effectiveness with which miners worked. Instead, the miners were angered by Ferdinand's *method* of directing them, his assumption of authority, and his challenge to the man whose method of supervision they preferred. One of the miners' distinctive reasons for supporting the strike was to eliminate the threat to Old Bull's authority. In the mine, Ferdinand played much the same role that Spiedman did on the surface; they both epitomized "close supervision" and both provided a focal point for resistance against it.

Aggression and its Barriers

The aggression provoked by increased close supervision, on top and bottom, might never have led to a strike unless certain specific conditions were present. Stated somewhat differently, certain mechanisms existed that inhibited responses other than aggression and, in fact, sanctioned its open expression. Three of these seem vital: (1) the scapegoat mechanism, (2) the "alertness" mechanism, and (3) the redrawing of primary-group boundaries.

The Scapegoat Mechanism. Many of the workers in the plant were closely identified with management and some of these held formal leadership posts in the union. The problem for these workers was to find a way to express aggression without seeming to direct it against management as a whole. Spiedman provided them with a convenient scapegoat, for he personified everything that the workers disliked; he was close supervision incarnate. Yet he was not a member of the main office team that really ran the Company, but merely its servant; nor was he a member of the local management to whom the workers would have to adjust after the strike was over. Thus one of the central demands advanced by the workers, after they walked out, was to "get rid of Spiedman." During the negotiations following the walkout, Bill Kayo asked management to remove Spiedman "*as an evidence of good faith* on the part of the Company," thus testifying to the symbolic role that the "practical engineer" had assumed. The miners also brought forth similar demands with regard to Ferdinand. In sum, both of these men, but especially Spiedman, provided the workers with targets for concerted aggression, without having to attack the Company as a whole. They could say, in effect, the Company was not too bad, just a few of its supervisors; thus the workers could still be "counted in," and a permanent cleavage with management would seem to have been avoided.

The "Alertness" Mechanism. We have seen that as work on the new machines progressed, management subjected workers to increased demands for "alertness." Initially, many of the workers had adjusted to the threatening plant tensions by "withdrawing" mentally, by setting emotional distance between themselves and objects in their situation. They said, as a takeoff man did, "The hell with it all, the only thing I'm going to watch from now on is the size of my paycheck; everything else can rot." The demand for increased alertness, however, disrupted this common mode of adjustment.

The workers complained that "the speed *keeps them on their toes* too much," as a wet end foreman said; "A man has to be *on the ball* more," in the words of a lift truck operator; or as a take-off operator said, "The new machinery made most of the jobs more difficult; you have to *pay more attention* to them." These remarks indicate the increased demands for alertness that were being made, as well as the workers' hostile reactions to them. It is important to notice the contradictory consequences of close supervision. On the one hand, close supervision encouraged many workers to utilize withdrawal mechanisms; on the other, however, the alertness-demands prevented successful withdrawal.

If we make our earlier assumption explicit, namely, that a withdrawing mode of adjustment is only one of a limited number of possible defense reactions, the other two probably being compliance-conformity and aggression, then the statistical frequency of the latter two is bound to increase. In short, the increased demands for alertness would seem to be another mechanism increasing the chances of an aggressive response to management.

Redrawing the Primary Group Boundaries. A third mechanism which, while it does not necessitate aggression, nevertheless *facilitates* it, was the workers' redefinition of the primary group situation. In the days before the first succession, but to a lesser extent afterwards, there had been a high degree of informality between workers and supervisors. This situation was recognized by the workers and supported with appropriate sentiments; most relevant of these was that aggression against supervisors was restrained. For example, the informal code as well as formal rules required that a worker tell his immediate supervisor about a complaint before going over his head. In part, this normative restraint against aggression derived from the mutual participation of workers and supervisors in an informal social organization, and was one of the workers' ways of reciprocating for management's conformity to the indulgency pattern.

But the tensions that had developed after the first succession, and the impersonal demotion of the old supervisors after the second succession, had destroyed workers' desires to be friendly with their supervisors. Workers no longer counted the supervisors among the members of their primary group. So long as the supervisors had been thought of as members of the workers' primary group, aggression could not be readily expressed toward them. In general, aggression is not defined as preferred behavior toward members of one's own informal or primary group; it tends to be viewed as permissible only when directed toward people with whom the aggressor does not have close personal ties. But after the supervisors had been read out of the workers' primary group, they then became legitimate targets for aggression; a barrier holding aggression back had fallen.

The Forms of Rationalization

The burden of the analysis up to this point has focussed on three factors, the technological innovations, the succession of the plant managers, and the strategic replacements among middle management. These pressures disrupted the worker-management relationship; for they led to close supervision which, in turn, violated parts of the indulgency pattern which had been an important element in maintaining stable labor relations. Schematically, the connections may be represented in the following way:

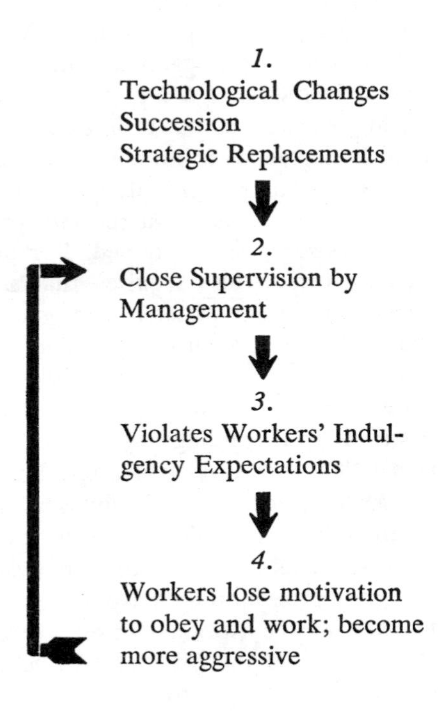

The "vicious circle" aspect of this chain is represented by the arrow from "4" leading back to "2." In other words, the more workers became aggressive toward their supervisors, and the more apathetic they became about their work, the more management employed close supervision. This, in turn, would ultimately reinforce the workers' apathy and aggression.

The three factors in phase "1," the technological and personnel changes, have certain similarities which now need to be made explicit. Each of them is, in effect, a form of "rationalization." The term "rationalization" refers to any mode of behavior which *seeks* to use limited resources in an economical way. As used here, rationalization does not mean the same thing as "efficiency," for efficiency is the result of a *successful* process of rationalization. To turn it the other way around, rationalization is behavior intended to make things efficient; but we should not commit ourselves to the optimistic assumption that rationalization always attains efficiency.

At any rate, it is evident that the new machines were introduced in the *hope* of attaining greater efficiency. But the succession and strategic replacements were also expressions of rationalization. The replacement of Peele by Landman was motivated by a desire to reduce wastage, improve labor discipline, and maintain a consistently higher output which was believed warranted by the new machines. Top management also felt that some of the middle management at the plant were not "on top of their jobs," and replaced them with men whom they *hoped* would be more efficient. In part, then, each of these three seemingly different patterns, technological change, succession, and strategic replacements, was an indication of a single, larger drive toward rationalization.

Rationalization might, of course, have been effectuated without using close supervision, perhaps by persuasion, rewards, or supportive techniques. But why did the drive to rationalize the plant employ close supervision rather than other administrative devices? In short, why did management use the stick rather than the carrot?

Rationalization as a Problem Solution

For management, rationalization was a solution to a problem. The problem was how to retain its share of the market in the postwar period with its heightened competition, and, ultimately, to expand the Company's position in the industry. The means management chose to employ were to cut unit-costs and to produce more and better gypsum board. These involved the three forms of rationalization which have been discussed.

In using these, however, other potential solutions were not perceived or were rejected. For example, management did not willingly entertain union suggestions that the speed of the new machines be set by joint negotiation. It is conceivable, though, that such a measure might have increased the worker's motivation to produce and, through this, lowered the unit-cost. Although a "human relations" program was adopted, it was never importantly developed. In general, management did not attempt to enlist greater cooperation from ordinary operatives with anything like the seriousness that it fastened upon the other solutions.

Why was it that management did not attack the problem of establishing a greater willingness to work in a more systematic and energetic way? One reason might be that it preferred solutions which were able to produce *predictable* consequences, while an effort to raise workers' motivation would be seen as having an *uncertain* outcome. This seems possible, but is not entirely satisfactory. The main office management did, after all, recognize that two of their problem solutions, the succession and the strategic replacements, could easily induce considerable worker dissatisfaction. Though management did not consider the consequences of these devices as adequately predictable, nevertheless, they did adopt them.

One common element in the techniques management did use was their susceptibility to top management *control*; for each of the solutions entailed a commitment to resources over which management believed itself to have greatest *control,* the machines and the managerial force. Management's drive for greater control was expressed in one of the reasons given for Peele's removal. "Under Peele every problem became a crisis," explained a main office executive. "Besides, he let Byta have his own way too much." Furthermore, each of these solutions was useable without modification of the status system, or more accurately, the managerial prerogatives secured by this system. In contrast, joint labor-management determination of the machines' speed was viewed by management as a status-threatening abridgment of its prerogatives, and was therefore resisted.

Management could not merely evaluate and choose its problem solutions in terms of their ability to realize the formal ends of increasing production and lowering unit-costs; they also required solutions which would be compatible with their status interests. They were, therefore, disposed to resist any solution which threatened their prerogatives and diminished their control over the situation, however much it might improve efficiency. Given management's fear that the workers were out to control the plant, which was discussed in the last chapter, management sought solutions which were safe as well as efficient.

In sum, management's status interest was one of the factors which channelled the path that rationalization of the plant was to take, leading it to defensive assertions of its authority, which conflicted with the deprecation of authority inherent in the indulgency pattern.

There were, of course, other factors disposing to the same result; one of the more obvious of these was the uncertain state of the market which, among other consequences, inhibited the use of generous wage inducements. The constriction of the *commodity* market led management to "get tough"; the poor state of the *job* market led management to feel that workers would have to accept this. In short, whether or not the pattern of rationalization takes the direction of close supervision depends, in further part, upon the state of the market.

The Role of Market Forces

In noting this, however, it should not be supposed that this was the only or most important way in which market forces contributed to the outbreak of the strike. For in many important ways, some of which will have to be considered in later chapters, the "market" as a complex arrangement of assumptions and behaviors was closely connected with the workers' expectations, and the possibility of their satisfaction or frustration.

It is characteristic of a market economy, for example, that pressure is exerted to withhold legitimation from claims which are not *explicitly* agreed upon by both parties, and thereby contractually established. Expectations to which explicit consent is not given tend to become regarded, in a market context, only as permissible or preferred patterns, even though in some other network of human relations they may be defined as prescribed or obligatory. It is in this sense that the workers' indulgency pattern, as a collection of non-legitimate expectations, is a product of market institutions.

Illustrating the effects of market assumptions within the plant, and of its role in fostering aggression toward management, were the many complaints about Digger, the personnel and safety manager replaced by Gudeguy. One such complaint follows:

> "This fellow Digger studied law—he's a shrewd fellow. The men don't like him. How would you feel if . . . here's an example: The office has parking space reserved for them, a roped or marked off spot. Digger had one of the foremen put a

man out there, to keep cars out of this space. A guy pulled in after 7. The foreman came out later and saw that the man he had placed there had left, so he had a man move this car. The kid [owner of the car] went out not knowing his car had been moved. He came to me and said, 'Ken, someone moved my car and scratched it.' There was a scratch all along one side. We went to the foreman who said we had to see Digger. Digger said, 'I didn't tell you anything about *moving* any cars out there.' When the kid started to talk, Digger said, "If you don't like the God-damned way we keep our cars in this lot, then keep your God-damned car in the lot across the street. *You don't pay for it.*' Whatever happens to our cars, they were not responsible. Digger said this. The foreman had to keep the cars out, yet Digger wanted the foreman to take the blame for him."

In this narrative, Digger holds that the burden of proving that a valid claim exists rests on the claimant, "the kid," and that he was not responsible for what the foreman did, illustrating the tendency to reject obligations not explicitly agreed upon. Moreover, the "kid's" claim is disputed, in a manner again revealing typical market assumptions, on the grounds that he did not pay for the use of the parking space.

Where explicit consent becomes the basic criterion of the legitimacy of a claim, then the legitimacy of all "customary" privileges is easily challenged. Given a power differential between two parties operating on such assumptions, the weaker party's expectations will be frequently violated. Where legitimation is based on explicit consent, there will be a tendency to defend claims by asserting that they had, indeed, been explicitly agreed to, in short, to speak of "broken promises." For such a formulation of grievances carries the implication that a claim had once been deliberately consented to, and was thus evidently legitimate. In brief, the incidence with which workers' expectations of management will be frustrated, as well as the formulation of subsequent grievances, is related to the operation of market assumptions.

Chapter Six

WHY THE STRIKE WAS A "WILDCAT"

THE DISCUSSION, so far, bears upon developments which could be present in *any* type of a strike, whether a "wildcat" or not. We have yet to explain the particular, or "wildcat," form of the strike. In order to do this, however, we need to explore and specify the meaning of the term "wildcat strike," for it cannot be assumed that this is a self-explanatory, simple, or unambiguous notion. Instead, a decision must be chanced as to which aspects of the complex reality denoted by a "wildcat strike" will be abstracted and subjected to analysis.

To do this, it will be helpful to turn to the most sophisticated, indeed the only deliberately sociological, analysis of wildcat strikes which has been made, that of Jerome Scott and George Homans, and examine the conception of "wildcat strikes" utilized there.[1] The first thing that may be noted upon inspection of this work is that the authors never make fully explicit their notion of a wildcat strike. This is not to say, however, that they give *no* indication of how they use this crucial term; for they do provide *implicit* specifications of the concept.

As theirs was a study of wildcat strikes in Detroit during World War II, they examine the hypothesis that Detroit's inadequate facilities might have frustrated workers, and speak of resultant "aggression in the form of strikes." In short, one aspect of a wildcat strike, for them, is "aggression." Secondly, they reject certain explanations of wildcat strikes, stating, "The usual explanation why men left their

[1] "Reflections on Wildcat Strikes," Jerome F. Scott and George C. Homans, *American Sociological Review*, June 1947, pp. 278-286.

work failed to explain why they stayed." In short, then, to Scott and Homans, a wildcat strike partly involved "aggression," and workers leaving their work.

What Is a "Wildcat Strike"?

This, however, fails to distinguish wildcat strikes from other types of strikes. There is one element, however, commonly believed to be characteristic of wildcat strikes, to which Scott and Homans do give attention. This is its apparently "unplanned" and "spontaneous" nature:

> One word about the so-called "spontaneity" of the strikes. An endless debate rages in Detroit over the question. Unlike many issues, *this knows no party lines*. Some union and *most* management people harp on the planned and unspontaneous nature of most wildcat strikes; some managers and a *good many* union people feel that most wildcat strikes are spontaneous. From the strikes we were told about, it appears that in almost all instances a wildcat strike presupposes communication and a degree of informal group organization. The strike has some kind of leadership, usually from within the group, and the leaders do some kind of planning, if only but a few hours or minutes ahead. *Whether this kind of behavior is "spontaneous" or "planned" is a quibble*. The interesting thing is not the question itself but what it implies about the people who raise it. Whether a person looks on a wildcat strike as "spontaneous," that is, unorganized, or as a deep and dark conspiracy, that is over-organized, he is probably showing his ignorance of informal group behavior in industry and elsewhere. [Our emphases—a.w.g.]

Rather than treating this pervasive interest in the "spontaneity" of wildcat strikes as an expression of ignorance about "informal groups," let us take it seriously and see what comes of it. For sociologists to content themselves with the statement that the discussion of "spontaneity" implies ignorance of "informal group behavior in industry," would be as inappropriate as a psychiatrist's castigation of a patient who was ignorant of theories dealing with the ego, id, or super-ego. In short, if the client is not always correct, he should at least be treated with respect: his symptoms have to be taken seriously.

The first thing that may be noticed is that these unionists and businessmen have, at least, been considering an important question, namely, what *is* a wildcat strike? Their dispute as to whether or not it is spontaneous can be taken as an effort to specify the meaning of such strikes. Now when people define a social problem, and a wildcat strike is certainly that, in a specific way, it does indeed, as Scott and Homans say, imply something about the people themselves. But ignorance aside, just what does the dispute about the wildcat strike's "spontaneity" imply about these people?

Notice, first, that the participants have stressed the way in which such strikes *originate*, that is, whether they were planned or spontaneous. Conversely, they deemphasized the things the strikes were about, the strike issues. Having noted this, it is now possible to proceed in two directions; that is, either by exploring the question of the neglected issues, or by more closely examining the dispute about the origins of wildcat strikes.

To consider the first alternative: What *are* the workers' demands in wildcat strikes? Homans and Scott transmit an important datum, namely, that relatively few of them involved wage questions. They further note that governmental statistics, which classify the issues involved in wildcat strikes, "are unsatisfactory and always include a large 'miscellaneous' column which defies easy description."

Since these statistics are usually classified with the interests of businessmen and labor leaders in mind, it may be inferred that wildcat strikes are about things, or involve issues, to which *this public* does not usually attribute much importance, or in which they are not usually interested. This provides one crude specification of what a wildcat strike is, to wit, that it is a strike involving issues ordinarily of "little interest" to labor and business leaders. Out of this a problem emerges: why have management and formal union leaders failed to focus on the issues involved in wildcat strikes; what about their frames of reference, or the workers' grievances, dispose industrial leaders to neglect these issues?

Returning to the dispute about the strikes' "spontaneity," let us examine its implications more closely. The content of the polemic about this question should not be loosely rendered. For example, counterposing "planning" versus "spontaneity," neglects to mention whether the planning is made by *formal* or *informal* leaders. The dispute can be considered a "quibble" only by implying that there is always some form of planning, whether by informal or formal leaders. In doing so, however, the real social issue is obscured; namely, whether or not the strikes were planned and led by the *formal union officials*. This was certainly no quibble, for on this question might hinge the possibility of legal action and court-imposed fines upon the union, to say nothing of its effect on the union's public relations. For this reason, the role of the *formal* union officials was the nub of the matter. If we bear this in mind, we cannot tell the participants, "Never mind the 'spontaneity' of the strikes, they were planned by *someone*; contemplate the role of the informal leaders." Management's contention was that these strikes were really planned, and there *was* a "party line" on this question, implicitly accusing the official union functionaries of striving to evade their responsibility for the strikes. By affirming the spontaneity of the strikes, the unionists were denying or attempting to evade this charge.

Now the question of whether or not a given strike has been led and sanctioned by the official union functionaries is an empirical one, and, of course, not to be decided by mere definition. The social scientist need not choose between the competing positions in characterizing a wildcat strike, but he *can* identify the variables concerning which there is a disagreement.

If the researcher finds that the managerial contention was correct, namely that formal union leaders employed hidden influence, then he may define his problem to be an analysis of the conditions which led to the use of concealed techniques of leadership by the formal leaders. If, contrariwise, and in accordance with the unionists' contention, the social scientist finds that formal union leaders have actually lost control of the situation, and that their official position no longer reflects their power, then he may take as his problem the reasons for this circulation of union leadership, asking how was it that informal leaders came to replace the formal.

In either event, however, analysis of the implications of the dispute over "spontaneity" is rewarding, for it leads to further specifications of a wildcat strike. In other words, a wildcat strike is now specifiable as either (a) a strike in which the formal union leaders pretend to have little control over the situation, but actually exert concealed influence on its course; this may be called the "pseudo-wildcat"; or a wildcat strike is specifiable as (b) one in which the formal union leaders have actually lost control and the strike is led by individuals whose position in the formal structure does not prescribe such a role for them, the "genuine wildcat."

Thus the problem is not merely one of being aware of the influence of informal leaders; rather it is a question of determining the conditions under which their influence can *supersede* that of the formal leadership. And even this unwarrantedly prejudges the facts. For the actual strike leaders in genuine wildcats may be people who hold some formal leadership post in the union, but a position which does not legitimate the degree of power which they assume in the strike. Formulated differently, the issue of "spontaneity" versus "planning" is a statement of critical symptoms, implicitly directing the researcher to attend to the relative role and *relationships* of different types of leaders.

So far, the standpoints of all the parties involved have been given consideration in our effort to specify the nature of a wildcat strike, *except those who actually go on strike*. Scott and Homans' work provides important assistance here. They state: "In the long run, a number of strikes seemed to stem from faulty communication. Workingmen would call it the 'run around.' They use that phrase when they feel that what they consider important is not in fact being treated as such by people in authority." Now this, of course, converges closely with our first specification of a wildcat strike, as one in which the issues involved are ordinarily of "little interest" to business and labor leaders.

More importantly, however, the "run around" suggests further that wildcat strikes constitute an expression of aggression against the *dilatory* manner in which workers' grievances are being dealt with. Our own examination of the strike symptoms, especially the complaints about the "pile up of broken promises," and the demand for redress from higher authorities, has already found this to be an element in the viewpoint of the strikers in the Oscar Center plant.

Scott and Homans at first emphasize that this is a consequence of "faulty communication." They write: "The need for communication becomes greater at a time when the lines of communication become *weaker* and *longer*." [our emphasis—a.w.g.] Growth of unions, increased government intervention, and the inexperience of middle management are held to impair the lines of communication between the workers at the bottom of the structure and the manager at its pinnacle. The underlying analogy employed here, however, is a thoroughly mechanical one, and the problem is conceived of as one similar to those which a telephone company has; that is, the defects are held to reside in the *lines* of communication. Using such a model, one expects inadequacies in the communication mechanisms, rather than in the *content* of what is being communicated. Thus, the telephone company looks to its lines or its power plant when a breakdown occurs, rather than to *what people have been saying to each other over their phones.*

It is apparent, of course, that the "communication lines" have been transmitting certain stimuli adequately. For example, wage grievances are effectively conducted by the existent communications apparatus, otherwise we would find them to be issues in wildcat strikes. But this is not typically the case. Even if a mechanical model is being used, this suggests another very different possibility—namely, that the communication mechanism in the factory was developed to handle different types of signals than those involved in the issues of wildcat strikes, just as a radio is not designed to receive television signals. In other words, it need not be that the communication mechanism has "broken down," as the "lines of communication have become weaker and longer," but rather that for certain purposes *they were never any good in the first place.* Homans and Scott verge on this possibility when they remark, "Yet the problem may not be just poor communication. In the automotive industry, people communicate well when it is a question of sales and engineering." Perhaps, they add, "it may be a problem of having a language in which to communicate. Or it may be that no one has time enough. . . ." But why is it, then, it must be asked, that people do have a language, and do have enough time to consider grievances entailing wages, hours, and union security?

The current emphasis on the pathological consequences of "growing" lines of communication appears to be an expression of what Homans has called elsewhere[2] the ideology of old-fashioned liberalism, one aspect of which is the suspicion of bigness in social organization. The focus on attenuated communication channels,

---

[2] George C. Homans, *The Human Group*, Harcourt, Brace and Co., 1950.

reciprocally isolating top and bottom, is reminiscent of the jaded paternalistic panacea which prescribed that if only workers and employers could come together in a face-to-face way, as they did in days of yore, all would be well in the world. Much of the recent concern over communications mechanisms has as its ideological content, it may be suggested, a plea for a return to the industrial womb.

To recapitulate: three specifications of wildcat strikes have been derived in the course of the above discussion. A wildcat strike has been held to be one in which:

1. The formally dominant union officials have lost power consonant with their positions to other persons in the union—the "genuine wildcat." Or: the formal union leaders have employed concealed influence in sanctioning and leading the strike—the "pseudo-wildcat." In regard to the case under study, the *first specification is correct.*

2. The issues involved are ordinarily of "little interest" to formal labor leaders and business managers.

3. Workers' aggression is directed at the dilatory manner in which their grievances are dealt with, i.e., the "run around."

This specification of wildcat strikes directs attention to the leadership dynamics, and it is to these we now turn.

On the Unanticipated Consequences of Being Conciliatory

The union leadership at the Oscar Center plant was divided into two, not completely stable, cliques. One of these was headed by Byta, the union president; the other was led by the union's vice-president, Izzaboss. Byta's clique included Crackery and Sodlen, who had been appointed union secretary over Izzaboss's objections. Though Crackery was no longer a formal union leader, he had once been looked upon as Byta's heir apparent; he and Byta were close to each other and handled union problems in a similar way.

The vice-president's clique was composed of Tenzman, the chief steward so closely involved in the events precipitating the strike, and two board plant workers. Together, both of these cliques comprised the official union negotiating and grievance committees. It is noteworthy that the three most influential local union leaders all had jobs which allowed them considerable physical mobility, enabling them to make and keep up informal contacts throughout the plant; Byta was an electrician, Izzaboss a welder, and Tenzman a painter. None of them was tied down to a machine.

At the very beginning of open conflict in the plant, Byta indicated a desire to withdraw from the situation, and to allow others to assume leadership. When, for example, the question had been raised as to whether foremen would be allowed to work, in connection with the changes which Spiedman was introducing, Byta had told management, "The next time this comes up I'm taking a walk." When the strike did come, a part of the union leadership, encouraged by Byta, had opposed an immediate walkout and insisted that the Company be given two hours' notice before the shutdown. They explained that, if there had been an immediate shutdown, all of the stucco would dry in the high-speed mixer and, as Sodlen said, "It would be hard for the men to clean out. It takes a couple of hours and it's hard to do." Sodlen continued:

> "We told the Company the guys were going to pull the switch. *We held them [the workers] back as long as we could.* We should have gone by grievance procedure rules. They lost their heads. A few guys got the committee all riled up. *I don't believe in my own heart it was right.*"

Moreover, shortly after the walkout, Sodlen had gone around tacking up makeshift signs on which were scrawled, "Unauthorized Walkout." Again, towards the end of the strike, at the crucial negotiations which took place the evening of the settlement, Byta had gone home early, muttering something about his wife being worried if he came home too late. The position of the president's clique was epitomized by Sodlen's remark, "There was a misunderstanding of the contract. It could have been talked over and worked out."

From their viewpoint, the strike was an unfortunate occurrence which could have been avoided. The attitudes of Izzaboss's clique were in sharp contrast with those of the president's. When, for example, at the end of the strike, we asked the wife of one of Izzaboss's followers whether her husband was going back to work that day, she replied, "Yes, but he would have liked to have stayed out more time. He would have liked more vacation." In the main, Izza-

represented the "traditionalist" position in defense of the pattern; Byta's clique largely expressed a "marketing out- ch sought to supersede the indulgency pattern.

ertain vital respects the leadership patterns described above plica of those which developed during the 1948 "quickie." as in the wildcat strike, Izzaboss emerged as an increasingly important leader; it was his name that the men called as they gathered around the negotiating room. At that time, also, Byta "made himself scarce," physically withdrawing from the scene of action.

Two questions need to be raised about this leadership pattern. First, why was it that Byta did *not want* to play the dominant leadership role during this strike, and conversely, why was Izzaboss *willing* to assume leadership? Secondly, what aspects of the *situation* made continued leadership difficult for Byta, constraining him to drop out, but made it possible for Izzaboss to forge ahead? In other words, to return to an important specification of a wildcat strike, what made it possible for Izzaboss to assume more power than his union office prescribed, and made it necessary for Byta to abdicate the power which his position permitted?

A crucial situational factor was the ineffectiveness of the union's grievance machinery prior to the strike. It has already been noted that the formal grievance machinery had broken down under the rising tide of grievances. As Crackery stated:

> "The union committee found that there was a pile up on grievances. There were a lot of grievances that the Company wasn't handling. . . . The Company wouldn't pay much attention to the grievances. They wouldn't fulfill their promises. They're supposed to write down their answers to a grievance when it's filed. They said we're thinking about it and they'd let you know one way or another."

Crackery's comments highlight the *Company's* role in the breakdown of the grievance machinery; this is an aspect of the situation to receive attention in a later chapter. Here, however, what is important is that the grievance machinery did not work; the question arises as to which clique was identified with its failure. Because the grievance machinery had been controlled by Byta's clique, until the strike, its failure was ascribed to Byta and his policies. The men complained that all they ever got from the committee were "prom-

ises," and they expected the committee to produce more th
In short, Byta's clique could not have led the strike, even had
wished to, since they were discredited because of their role in
grievance committee. They could not have led the strike because they
were not being followed.

An important reason why the grievance machinery broke down, as well as a reason why Byta's clique was *not* motivated to lead the strike, was the fact that they did not regard the grievances which they had to represent as legitimate ones. Crackery's comments reveal their conflicts clearly:

> Personally, I get along with Spiedman . . . I used to call him anything I want, and he can call me anything he wants to. As far as I know, he [Spiedman] had never picked on any man except Tenzman. His job was to speed up the machine and when Tenzman complained, he told him to mind his own business. [Grievances against foremen are] sometimes placed by a man who doesn't even know the foremen. They see a foreman working and boom! It is not always the foremen's fault. Sometimes it's the fellow who puts in the grievance."

Since Byta's clique was ambivalent toward the workers' grievances and doubtful of their legitimacy, they did not "push them"; they could not represent them to management with anything like the strong affect that their followers felt. In other words, Byta's conciliatory attitude toward the grievances actually did much to *prevent* conciliation between management and labor. For top management had few systematic ways of assessing the workers' feelings other than through the watered expression which Byta's clique gave them. Insofar as Byta and his followers viewed the strike as an expression of doubtfully legitimate grievances, they could not, as Sodlen put it, believe in their own "hearts" that the strike was "right." In brief, they did not want to lead the strike, even if they would have been followed by the workers, because they were not convinced of its legitimacy.

The Byta clique's unwillingness to assume the strike leadership seems to go much deeper than these value-conflicts, and was also rooted in their character structures. The same thing may, of course, be said for the *willingness* of Izzaboss's clique to take over the leadership. The different personality needs of the men in these two cliques can, to some extent, be gauged from Thematic Apperception Tests which were given to Crackery and Izzaboss, the former being close to and prominent in Byta's clique, the latter being the leader of his own clique. The TAT results were analyzed by three specialists,[3] who were told only that the protocols which they examined came from individuals of a given age and sex, that they were both leaders, and worked at a plant in a nearby town. A specific focus was given to their analysis, since we asked them to concentrate on the manner in which the respondents handled their aggression and conceived of authority. They were not, of course, given any indication of the writer's hypothesis concerning the specific differences they might find in the two men. The results of their analysis are summarized below.

Crackery's TAT gave evidence of a "more highly developed super-ego than did Izzaboss's. Crackery seems to have had a rather strict, conventional upbringing. While he may sometimes chafe against it, on the whole he probably remains within its boundaries." Crackery stresses certain things having no counterpart in Izzaboss's protocol. For example, speaking of one of the TAT pictures, he remarks, "If he's committed a wrong, there's some way he can make amends . . . that is, if he's got any character at all." The TAT analyst comments, "Here Crackery expresses a firm middle class moral attitude, which is fortified by respectful attitudes toward parents and parent surrogates."

Unlike Izzaboss, Crackery had a fairly strict, conventional super-ego, which was quick to punish him should he depart from its prescriptions. Crackery has a "tremendous amount of repressed and unexpressed hostility. There are few references to deviant behavior in Crackery's protocols. Where they occur, they are surrounded with expressions of guilt and vagueness."

Crackery's aggression was held in check by his super-ego. It could escape only in "impulsive outbursts," which are followed by feelings of guilt. In contrast, Izzaboss was "an individual who appears

---

[3] Two of these, Frances and Nathan Shenfeld, are clinical psychologists who worked together. The other, Victor Barnouw, is a cultural anthropologist. See V. Barnouw, *Acculturation and Personality Among the Wisconsin Chippewa*, Memoir #72 of the American Anthropological Association, October 1950.

to be independent, aggressive. . . . [He] does not allow the environment to get the better of him." Izzaboss would "be more likely to give way to aggressive impulses and deviant behavior. . . . [He] is more aggressive than Crackery."

Crackery was more of an indecisive person because of his ambivalences. "One of these ambivalences involves a conflict between passivity or active expression of aggression." Similarly, "Crackery sees people as passive, not expressing hostility."

It was indicated by Crackery's TAT that his rebellious tendencies were greatly suppressed and that, unconsciously, conflicts with authority were perceived by him as being his own fault, leading him to "make amends," and that he possessed strong inclinations toward dependency. Such a character structure, and Byta's and Sodlen's appeared similar in this respect, does not want to engage in aggressive behavior toward authority figures, least of all in actions which were not subject to unmistakable legitimation nor supportable by other authorities, such as the top regional union officials.

The men in Byta's clique had strong convictions about the strength of authority and had needs to defer to it. In discussing Spiedman's "swearing" with Sodlen he remarked, "You should never swear at a *supervisor*; you must show respect where respect is due." This clique looked to authority as a source of security, hoping, for example, that the Lakeport management would resolve the plant tensions for them. Thus Sodlen had gone to the Lakeport office on his own initiative, sometime before the outbreak of the wildcat, to request that they do something to remedy the situation. They were men whose security came from acceptance by authority figures. In Byta's case, for example, he came to the plant originally under the "protection" of "Old Doug," and when Doug died, Byta sought to use his union position to extract personal acceptance from Peele, quickly changing from a "militant" to a "cooperative" union leader when this was accomplished.

In contrast, Izzaboss was strongly independent, and unafraid to express aggression toward authorities. It was therefore possible for Izzaboss to lead the strike without feeling guilty. Izzaboss's uninhibited and sustained ability to rebel could also enable ambivalent workers to resolve their own conflicts about the expression of aggression, whereas Byta's conflicts on that score could only intensify the ambivalences which existed among some men.

Summary

The following diagrams give some summary indication of the factors disposing Byta's clique to withdraw from leadership and inducing Izzaboss's clique to assume it.

Byta's Clique

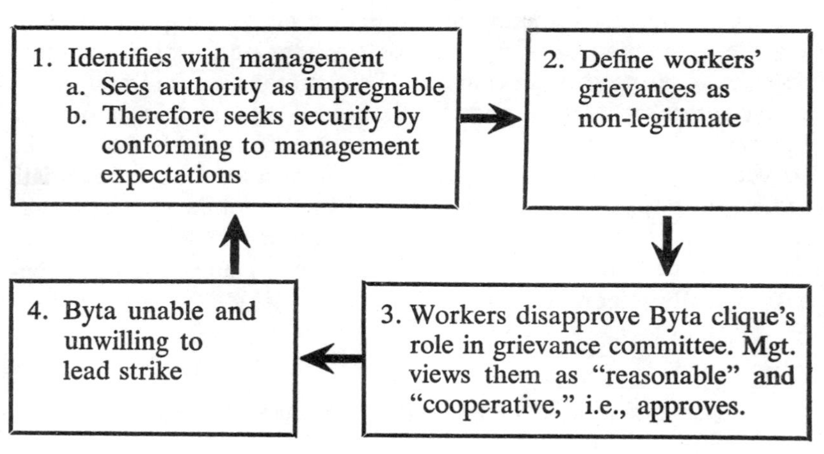

Izzaboss's Clique

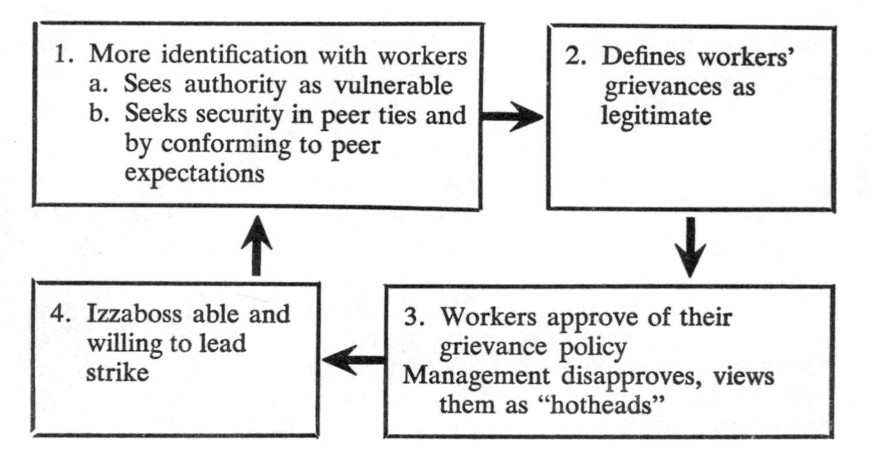

These factors give some indication of why the formal leadership of the union, the men who were legitimately empowered to lead a strike, were supplanted by union leaders who had no such formal authority. Moreover, it is in part due to their doubts concerning the legitimacy of the workers' grievances that the formally dominant union leadership had "comparatively little interest" in the issues which precipitated the strike.[4]

A prevalent conception among industrial sociologists, concerning the communications function of trade unions, would therefore seem to be in need of amendment. The current view suggests that a union serves as a mechanism *expediting* communication from the low-ranking operatives to the top managerial staff. This may be so with respect to certain types of communication but, as our data indicates, it is not always the case. When the formal union leaders are oriented toward managerial expectations, and when they, therefore, view certain of the workers' grievances as non-legitimate, they may actually impair upward communication.

Leadership Circulation and Market Pressures

The competition and circulation of union leadership in the plant were connected, in ways of varying complexity, with the market institutions in the larger economy. It is obvious, for example, that the union-management contract—as a part of the market complex—directed attention to certain types of issues, simultaneously detracting it from others. Thus, in the 1948 negotiations, discussions were held on wages only because the contract allowed no other issue to be raised at that time. It will be remembered that in the wildcat strike, Byta's clique conceived of it as due, in part, to "misunderstanding of the contract," indicating that they were using the contract as a baseline in terms of which to judge the issues. This orientation to the contract, to the issues which it defined as legitimate, and to

---

[4] The circulation of leadership, characteristic of the wildcat strike, is thus consonant with the hypothesis that "a leader will be accepted by group members to the extent that he helps them achieve their goals." Donald C. Pelz, "Leadership Within a Hierarchical Organization," *Journal of Social Issues*, Vol. VII, No. 3, 1951, p. 55.

the devices which it installed for the remedy of grievances, impaired the influence of Byta's clique, and helped Izzaboss, with his greater receptivity to a wider range of claims, to assume leadership.

Market factors also seemed to contribute to the motivation of those who were engaged in the competition for union leadership. When Byta had first come to the plant, he did so at the suggestion of "Old Doug" who had led him to expect rapid ascendancy. After Doug died, and Peele succeeded him, Byta sought and assumed the presidency of the local in the hope, which he explicitly admitted, that this would once again bring him to top management's attention. Later on, he used his presidency to extract an "understanding," relating to personal preferment, from Peele. Byta had used his union position to improve his job opportunities and to develop his career. This was done in conformity with the Company practice of promoting union leaders to supervisory positions. In sum, opportunities on the job market could be enhanced by holding a union position and were an element in the competition for union leadership.

This came out even more clearly in Izzaboss's ascent in the union. Following the end of the strike, Izzaboss called the Company's labor relations director and asked to see him. As the labor relations director related the story:

> "Just to show you the kind of a guy Izzaboss is, after the strike he called from his home in Zema. We live in West Borealis. He asked my wife and me to meet his wife and him for a drink. So we went in and had a drink . . . Izzaboss knows he'd do a good job of running the mine, therefore he helps Old Bull and Ferdinand cut each other's throat. Izzaboss wants to be either president of the union or head of the mine . . . probably mine head."
>
> (*Will Byta get the promotion he's been expecting for a long while now?*)
>
> "I don't know. Izzaboss will first, probably."

Another relevant characteristic of a market economy is that the distribution of rewards is but little influenced by the doctrinal or ideological purity of the recipient. "Results," or the ability to "produce" count decisively in this economy. While they are doubtless of great significance also in the totalitarian states, considerations of doctrinal reliability noticeably constrict the distribution of rewards.

Thus, in Nazi Germany, Mr. Einstein's work and person went unrewarded and were, in fact, proscribed, despite the international recognition accorded him. In like manner, under the bureaucratic "socialism" in the U.S.S.R. there is no scholarly or scientific activity too abstruse to claim exemption from continual pressure to manifest and reaffirm doctrinal orthodoxy.

In a market economy still moored to liberal commitments, however, there is no official ideology which is legally sanctioned and, in consequence, programmatic dissidence among workers is not yet heresy. Management has only the most diffuse political commitments to one side or another in an inner-union controversy. It is willing to do business with a union faction of almost any political hue, so long as it is a legal one, and is willing and able to meet the contractual obligations which is assumes.

An interesting illustration of this was main office management's attitude toward the former regional representative of the international union, Garten. At the time our researches began, the region was experiencing a well publicized and enthusiastic Red-hunt into the ranks of local union functionaries. Garten was one of those under attack as a Communist, by his own national headquarters. Main office management was concerned lest this internecine strife ripple into the local unions with which they dealt. The managerial staff gave quiet support to Garten because they felt he had been reasonable in his demands and had fostered cooperative labor relations with them.

On several occasions, also, other accounts were given by main office executives of how Communists employed by them changed into friendly and cooperative workers. As one Lakeport executive said:

> "When we first decided to open a plant in ———, everybody was against it. We went ahead and haven't had any trouble since. I remember when the plant first opened. There was a trouble maker named ——— who disrupted most of the time. He was the only real Communist and radical I ever met. Well, our plant really tamed him. The last I saw of him, he told me he had taken the job with the intention of disrupting, but that our way of operating had convinced him that such activity was bad. When the ——— plant was awarded a Navy 'E', he was the proudest man in the place."

The main point here is that, for management in a market economy, political ideology as such is not a crucial criterion of the acceptability of a partner to a contractual agreement. A group of unionists who champion a dissident program may expect to be dealt with by management, providing that they can gain leadership. Thus market assumptions and arrangements provide an elastic framework in which leadership competition and circulation can take place among unionists. This need not, however, be the case where a market economy, with its vestiges of "laissez-faire," is being supplanted by an "administered economy" and is thereby exposed to the political and ideological preferences of the state.

Chapter Seven

MANAGEMENT — WILLING BUT UNABLE

IN THE LAST CHAPTER, it was shown that some of the formal union leaders served to bottleneck the workers' grievances, impairing management's ability to know of and satisfy their expectations, and thereby contributing to the breakdown in worker-management relationships. In this chapter, we shall look at *management's* role, to see how their behavior also contributed to the conflict.

Even though Byta's clique inhibited the expression of workers' grievances through the grievance committee, it is still possible that management could have learned about the critical issues, in good time, from *unofficial* sources. In the following pages, therefore, three problems will be sifted:

(1) How well was management actually informed of the workers' real attitudes or "state of mind," regardless of the sources through which this information came? Did they perceive the situation as one in which open conflict might appear? These questions are akin to the conventional inquiries about the state of the communication mechanisms; here, however, emphasis shall be placed on the managerial node of the communication network.

(2) How did management feel about the precipitating grievances? Did they want to solve them? In other words, even if management had known about the grievances, and had recognized them to be "dangerous," it is still possible that they might not have *wished* to alleviate them.

(3) Suppose, however, that management did know about the grievances, did recognize their danger, and did want to remedy them. Was there anything in management's situation which might have prevented them from acting effectively? Knowledge and motivation

aside, was there anything which *constrained* management to behave in ways which neglected the workers' grievances?

DID MANAGEMENT KNOW?—THE COMMUNICATIONS PROBLEM

Several aspects of this strike apparently lend weight to the viewpoint which ascribes importance to communication blocks in bringing about labor-management cleavages. Among the most prominent was the visit which Sodlen made to a main office production executive, several months before the strike. Sodlen was received with seeming reluctance by this man. Sodlen was invited to come after he was asked for, and gave, assurances that he wished to talk only about personal matters. During the meeting, however, Sodlen *did* describe the critical situation in the plant, speaking of the "powderkeg that was set."

Certain features of this event appear to suggest communication blocks. First, the visit was taken on Sodlen's own personal initiative and is, perhaps, indicative of his and other workers' feelings that the formal communication channels were inadequate. Secondly, management expressed some reluctance to talk with him, unless he could assure them that his visit did not concern official union matters, though, of course, everyone knew that it would touch upon these. Seemingly, workers' communications to management were inhibited, as was management's receptivity to them.

But this is much too simple, and more careful examination of the event reveals complexities. However doubtful Sodlen was about the adequacy of the formal communication mechanisms, notice that he did conceive it possible for him, as an ordinary worker, to talk with the man who was production manager over some 25 plants. However cautious management was to define their meeting in a publicly acceptable way (i.e., as "personal business"), the hard fact is that they did meet. Not only that, they did communicate about plant business, and not merely about personal matters. Top management *had* been informed that the plant situation was critical. As the labor relations director commented, "We've been struggling against time since last January."

Communication concerning the uneasy state of the plant had arrived. Whether top management understood this to refer to a situation in which open conflict could appear is much less certain. There are several reasons for doubting that top management did understand the communication in this way. First, top management tended to feel that they could rely on Byta's clique to keep things "cooperative" at the Oscar Center plant; Sodlen's visit to the main office only strengthened their reliance on Byta's group. Secondly, top management did not fully realize the degree to which Byta's leadership had been jeopardized by his very cooperation with management. Management still had a lingering hope that Byta's group could keep things under control. Third, and finally, though the labor relations director claimed that management had been "working against time" to rectify what it recognized as a critical plant situation, nothing was actually done which would confirm this. Summing up, management did have *some* indications of what might happen in the plant, though it does not seem that it clearly perceived the danger as imminent.

Management's Motivation

To ask whether management wanted the strike is much like asking whether most people want war. In neither case is the answer, "yes." This, however, is not the only relevant query concerning motivation. A more decisive one is whether the participants want to remedy the grievances which could precipitate conflict, and in the name of which the battle can be joined.

There can be little doubt that management did not want the strike. Their prompt efforts to stop it once it had begun, their genuine unhappiness at its occurrence, testify to their motives here. No evidence exists, however, that they were willing to act upon the *specific* grievances which became the strike issues. On the contrary, management's conception of these grievances actually inhibited their motivation to mitigate them.

The Company's approach to workers' grievances was not an *ad hoc* one, however ambivalent and vacillating it was, but it was generalized, and deliberately expounded in its Labor Relations Manual. Initially, this manual emphasizes the importance of flexibility and a willingness to cope with "unusual" grievances:

> "The Plant Manager should guard against strictly legalistic interpretations [of the contract]. He should interpret the contract in a clear and common sense manner, with reasonable flexibility and fairness in handling unusual matters within the intention of the agreement."

"Common sense," of course, is a matter of expectations and values, and can provide an effective basis for decision only where it is unambiguous. One of the problems here was that there were conflicting "common senses" at work; for example, the tension between "seniority" and "efficiency" in the matter of demoting the old foremen. The manual then proposes that a distinction be made between two types of workers' demands, "complaints" and "grievances."

> "Where plant labor agreements provide for compulsory arbitration as the final step in the grievance procedure, Plant Managers should use care to differentiate between employee complaints and employee grievances."

A "grievance" is a demand made by the workers which can be legitimated with reference to the contract, and therefore has a valid claim to management action:

> "As a general rule . . . it would be well for all plants to recognize as grievances only those questions which arise out of the application or interpretation of various clauses of the contract."

Contrariwise, a "complaint" is a *non*-legitimate workers' demand, including:

> "Subjects such as *election and placement* of supervisors, type of product manufactured, *schedule of operations*. However, they are not the type of complaint that management is willing to consider as grievances for the purpose of arbitration."

"Complaints" were to be dealt with in the following manner:

> "As a matter of good employee relations, the Plant Manager should *talk over* with the union committee any complaint raised. If the complaint is regarding a matter which is of no concern [sic] to the union, this should be pointed out in a *proper manner*."

Briefly, then, a "grievance" was a potentially legitimate demand; legitimate because it bore upon and was resolvable by reference to the contract, while a "complaint" was non-legitimate. As a consequence, some of the very issues which precipitated the strike, the changing speed of the machine, the demotion of the old supervisors and their replacement with new ones, were defined by management as non-legitimate. These might be "talked over," but plant managers were cautioned against taking official cognizance of them. Thus, however unwilling management was to have a strike occur, it had defined many of the grievances which precipitated it in a way that tied their own hands. Management's willingness to remedy the grievances was impaired by its conviction that they were unjust.

The above account purports only to explain why management's motivation to resolve the grievances was undermined; but there still remains a further question. For if management did not want to alleviate these grievances, why didn't it *reject* them in a *forthright* manner? Why, instead, did they pursue a policy of postponement which further compounded the original grievances, so that workers added to their initial roster, complaints about the "pile up" of broken promises, the "run around"?

What were some of the factors involved in management's indecisive behavior? As one element, the Labor Relations Manual indicated that "complaints" had to be rejected carefully, and that workers were to be told in a "proper manner" when their claims were not officially negotiable. Moreover, the plant manager was constrained to thread his way cautiously between Charybdis and Scylla; between "legalistic" interpretations of the contract which violate common sense, and the danger of allowing infringements of managerial prerogatives.

Pressed between these conflicting tendencies, managerial indecision must be taken as a normal response to mutually inhibitory directives. Moreover, since the negotiability of a claim in any given case was often uncertain, local management often had to have recourse to main office legal experts. This, however, was a time-consuming process; while, in point of time, it may not have actually been "long," it often seemed that way to aggrieved workers champing for redress.

In the meantime, workers would be encouraged to "talk their problems over." Even if local management knew it would have to reject a claim, and even if it knew it could do so on its own authority, the modern labor relations procedures to which the Lakeport management was oriented prescribed a "cathartic" session. "Let the employee talk himself out," instructs the Manual. "This in and of itself will frequently satisfy him," it suggests. Thus the installation of "non-directive" methods as a device of labor relations may, in effect, come to serve as a scientific warrant for a managerial refusal to make consequential decisions.

Both local and main office management did not wish to decisively reject the workers' grievances for fairly obvious reasons. For one thing, they feared the consequences, recognizing that such a rejection would only further intensify labor-management cleavages. Moreover, they often felt that the workers' complaints had a certain justification, even if they were not contractually compelling. Thus, as we saw, there was dissatisfaction and uneasiness even among management concerning the decision to demote the old foremen.

Management's policy of postponement, therefore, resulted in part from a conflict in its own motivations and values. On the one side, there existed motives for rejection of the workers' complaints; on the other, there was fear of the consequences if the claim was rejected, or a nagging suspicion that the workers might be right. Motives for rejection clashed with motives for acceptance. The "run around," therefore, is a mode of adapting to claims, which strives to compromise conflicting motives by overtly committing the actor to *neither* side. Like the compromise solutions so familiar to psychopathologists, such a solution further intensifies the tensions from which it emerges.

Constraints on Managerial Action

It was shown that the distinction between "complaints" and "grievances" was a consequential one, and it needs to be asked why management made such a distinction. Stated differently, why did management strive to limit "grievances" only to "those questions which arise out of the application or interpretation of various clauses of the contract"? The Labor Relations Manual indicates that management did so in order to safeguard their status-prerogatives:

> "Contracts that contain compulsory arbitration clauses limit the questions which may be arbitrated to those arising out of interpretation or compliance with the contract. . . . If a question arising out of the *Company's exercise of its normal managerial functions* is treated as a regular grievance the union might successfully claim that the Company waived its right *not to arbitrate* the particular question." [our emphases—a.w.g.]

In effect, the Manual states that there are certain questions which management will not arbitrate, that is, "complaints," because to do so would threaten its "normal managerial functions." Here the Company emphasizes close conformity to contractual specifications, despite its earlier injunction against "legalistic" interpretations.

Management's behavior is oriented to the defense of its status position. They anticipate that workers will not respect or acknowledge that there are certain managerial rights which are beyond negotiation; they do not expect that workers will draw a line to their demands, saying, "So far and no further will we go." In short, management conceived of workers' demands as insatiable.

Another dimension of what a "complaint" is now becomes manifest; it is in the main a worker's demand which threatens to modify status relationships between workers and management, and which would deprive management of its traditional powers. The distinction between "complaints" and "grievances" serves to demarcate and define the former as non-legitimate, thus operating as a mechanism of status defense for management. Management's unwillingness to remedy the grievances involved in the wildcat strike was thus embroiled in its effort to safeguard its status.

Management's need to clearly define its status prerogatives and to put them beyond negotiation derives, in part, from certain characteristics of the market economy within which it operated. In a market economy, the status system, and the legitimate expectations of the parties involved, are registered in the contract and in the interpretations placed upon it; over time, these establish a cumulative body of precedent. In such a status system, there is the ever present possibility that any attribute of the participants' status may be subject to negotiation, and thus to modification—at least within the confines established by constitutional law or other legal prohibitions. Under such a status system, there is always the possibility of a "creeping" modification of the statuses involved, of an inch-by-inch transformation of the status duties and rights. Inasmuch as status rights are defined by the contract, the first line of status defense is the contract; similarly, the tendency to indulge in "legalistic" interpretations of the contract corresponds, and is a response, to the possibility of a "creeping" deterioration of one's status position.

In summary: There were certain things management desired to exempt from negotiation or arbitration, things they conceived of as their status rights, such as promoting or demoting supervisors, or regulating the speed of production. These rights had to be safeguarded in a distinctive type of threatening situation. That is, due to the market and contract character of the status system, there might occur a "creeping" infringement of their rights and a gradual deterioration of their status position. The way in which management defended its position in such a situation was to define workers' demands in a dichotomized manner. Certain of the demands, the "grievances," were accorded potential legitimacy; the legitimacy of the other demands, the "complaints," was *a priori* denied. Since many of the issues involved in the wildcat strike fell into the latter category, the complaints, management was unwilling to resolve them. For these reasons, then, the market-contract status system was a barrier inhibiting managerial action which might have obviated the strike.

The Decision-Making Process and Market Forces

As seen in the section on "Management's Motivation," one of the contributants to the breakdown in labor-management relations was the *indecision* of the managerial staff. In what ways was this indecision related to involvement in a market economy, or, more broadly, how is involvement in a market economy consequential for the decision-making process? Generally, there were a number of ways in which such involvement served to retard and slow down decision-making:

(1) Operation in a market economy with its contract-binding relationships disposes the participants to be *aware of the committing character* of a decision, and to think of it as a consequence-generating act. It is culturally prescribed that decision-making in a market economy should be a matter of deliberation rather than spontaneity; it is conceived of as a calculated rather than an "expressive" action.

In a market economy, the making of a decision typically constitutes a contractual commitment which is legally enforceable, and which may not be revoked despite changes in the contracting parties' ability to meet the obligations they have incurred. Thus the participant in a market relation is constrained to caution as the classical injunction, *caveat emptor*, signifies. A sensitivity to the consequences of a decision generates efforts to assess these *in advance*, thus inhibiting the speed with which the decisions may be made.

(2) There are certain results that flow from the decision-making process which are peculiarly important in a market economy, namely, the pecuniary consequences. Decisions therefore tend to be translated into their pecuniary implications wherever this is possible. An illustration of this was the procedure followed by the Lakeport office whenever they received the union's demands for the regular contract negotiations. One of the first things done with these demands was to translate them into their dollars and cents equivalents.

On one such set of demands, for example, there was a pencilled note indicating what each demand would cost the Company. Thus, "one additional paid holiday" would cost $2,892.33; "leave with pay for death in immediate family" was estimated for the forthcoming year as $8,676.89; "a wage increase of 15 cents per hour" would cost $102,616.80. Notice that the cost translations were not merely made to the nearest dollar, but also to the nearest penny.

Given such an emphasis on translating workers' claims into their monetary equivalents, pressure is exerted to facilitate decisions on those claims for which the costs are calculable, but to *impede* decisions on claims where this is difficult or impossible. It will be recalled that many of the claims involved in the wildcat strike, for example, the "working foremen" or supervisors "overstepping their bounds," were precisely claims for which no cost translation was possible, even if management had deemed them legitimate. This seems particularly important in understanding wildcat strikes. For, typically, they do *not* involve a wage issue, whose costs can be more easily calculated in advance, but involve intangibles which retard decision-making.

(3) A market economy engenders extreme sensitivity to the *competitive position* of the enterprise. Decisions must, therefore, be weighed in terms of their possible effects on the Company's position in its industry. As a result, it becomes important to align an enterprise's decisions with those which a competitor is contemplating or making. In modern labor relations, this emphasis finds its way even into the participants' language habits, eliciting references to the "pattern" of union settlements that are emerging, and to the importance of "keeping in line" with them. Unless this is done, of

course, a company may find itself forced to "price its products out of the market," and driven into a marginal position.

As a reflection of these pressures, the Labor Relations Manual prescribes that:

> "In determining what constitutes a fair wage, the Plant Manager should give *first* consideration to rates paid by competing firms in the same area. It is the Company policy to pay rates equal to those paid by principal competition located in the area."

Typical of the comparative cost analyses frequently made by the Company was one of the differential costs per ton of gypsum. The report notes the difference in bonus plans used by the Company, in comparison with its competitors, and recommends that the Company "get in line."

The relevant consideration here is that involvement in a market economy, with its concomitant sensitivity to the enterprise's competitive position, often impedes a company's decision until a competitor makes his decision. Not uncommonly, each is in turn waiting for the other to make the first decision. It is interesting in this connection, to note that in the 1948 negotiations the Company made an acceptable offer only after one of its competitors in the area had first granted a wage increase.

(4) At least one other characteristic of a market economy contributes to friction in the decision-making process and engenders hesitation. This is the unpredictability of the state of the market and its susceptibility to major changes without warning. A decision made during one set of market conditions may generate obligations which persist until, or only come due in, a period characterized by very different market circumstances. Thus in 1948, when the Company first began its rationalization of the plant, many workers were concerned about a possible decline in their overtime work, and a loss in their take home pay. Despite the dangers of such fears among workers, main office management could not provide clear-cut assurances that the work week would not be reduced. To guarantee a work week premised knowledge of future market conditions, and involved the assumption that the demand for the Company's product would not sink beneath the existent level. In a market economy these assumptions cannot be readily granted. More generally, decisions

often have to wait for the "clarification of market conditions" to avoid a loss in meeting obligations which come due under changed market circumstances.

To sum up, involvement in a market economy inhibits the decision-making process in the following ways: (1) by defining decision-making as a dangerous situation, caution comes to be the culturally prescribed attitude with which decisions are made; (2) by emphasizing cost calculability, decisions about workers' claims which have *no* cost translation tend to be inhibited; (3) by orienting the managerial staff to the decisions of its competitors, the enterprise's own decisions tend to be held up; (4) by the unpredictability and changeability of the market, heightened caution is induced.

Those macroscopic aspects of the market to which we have referred are in no way esoteric. What we have attempted to do, however, is to take these commonly recognized features of market institutions and to indicate their bearing on the internal relations of a small factory group, showing, in particular, their role in generating a complaint peculiar to wildcat strikes, the "run around."

Chapter Eight

THE REDUCTION OF TENSION IN THE PLANT

AFTER SEVERAL WEEKS of negotiations between the Company and the union a settlement was finally reached which the workers accepted. The strike was ended on the basis of the following terms which were incorporated in a memorandum of understanding:

1. "(a) Spiedman will finish his job (at the plant in another city to which he had been sent during the strike) before returning to Oscar Center. This will require at least three to four weeks. (b) Upon his return [he] will have to work through top [plant] management rather than superseding management."

2. "(a) Ferdinand will be put in charge of mine development, air, and water problems, etc. (b) He will not be in charge of a production gang."

3. "(a) The union and the Company will get together to work out a practical understanding concerning foremen working." (b) The arrangement later agreed upon specified that management was not to run the board machinery faster than related machinery allowed. That is, management was to install new take-off and other machinery, so that the speed of the board machine would not be greater than that of other machinery into which it fed lath.

4. "All union stewards will be required to get the permission of their foreman before leaving his department."

THE LATENT MEANING[1] OF THE AGREEMENT

---

[1] The notion of "latent meaning" is one which we have implicitly relied upon throughout this study, and will be used extensively in the present chapter. The latent content of an idea, or a proposition, are its implicit meanings when interpreted in terms of a frame of refer-

A. *Delimiting spheres of authority and competence:* In effect, item 2 of the agreement does the following: first, it reaffirms the sphere of competence of the mine superintendent, Old Bull, and secondly, it establishes a new office with a limited sphere of competence and authority, dealing only with air and water problems in the mine, to which Ferdinand is assigned.

Similarly, item 1(b) is a directive defining the relationship between the traveling engineer, Spiedman, and the local plant management. It reaffirms the plant manager's right to sole access and exclusive authority over production workers, indicating that the traveling engineer does *not* have authority for direct and self-initiated contact with workers. Provision 4 of the agreement further specifies the authority of the foreman over stewards within his department. These several provisions, then, served to specify and delimit spheres of authority and competence in the plant.

B. *Reinforcing Centralized Organization:* The delimitation of authority in the plant was done in such a way as to strengthen the *system* of subordination and dominance along *hierarchical* lines. For example, item 1, in effect, reasserts "one man" administration of the plant, subordinating the traveling engineer to the plant manager. Item 2 frees Old Bull from Ferdinand's challenge and competition, installing the former as undisputed head of the mine. In short, the lines of subordination were clarified and centralization was strengthened.

C. *Extension of Formal Rules:* The delimitation of authority and the reinforcement of the hierarchical system within the plant took place through the extension of formal rules. Item 4, for example, provided for greater managerial control over union stewards by installing a general rule to that effect. Still another rule is indicated in item 4(b) which directs supervisors not to speed up the board machine to a point where other machines will be unable to handle the work.

D. *Reinforcing Impersonal Attitudes:* Management's agreement to keep Spiedman out of the plant for three or four weeks after the

---

ence which takes cognizance of elements in the situation to which the participants are oriented, even though they are not fully aware of them. Cf., the essay by Abraham Edel, in M. Farber (editor), *Philosophy for the Future,* Macmillan Co., 1949.

strike represented a tacit acceptance of the complaints about his "swearing." It was a way of punishing Spiedman for violating managerial prescriptions which called for "businesslike," or "cool-headed" treatment of subordinates. In short, the utilization of officially prescribed, impersonal modes of behavior was strengthened by the terms of the agreement.

Summing up, then, the agreement which ended the strike did so by way of delimiting spheres of competence and authority, centralizing the hierarchical system, extending the sway of formal rules, and reinforcing the propriety of impersonal attitudes within the plant. Since each of these developments is an aspect of *bureaucratic* administration, we can say, in a summary way, that the defense mechanism used to restore labor-management relations to their equilibrium was increased "bureaucratic" organization. How did this happen? Why was increased bureaucratization used to reduce the tensions between workers and management? What gains were derived or anticipated from the use of this pattern of defense?

Some Functions of Bureaucratization

It may have been noticed that items 1 and 2 both restricted Spiedman's and Ferdinand's authority in one specific direction: they curtailed their direct interaction with the line or production workers. Thus Ferdinand was removed to a task involving little line authority and became a technical specialist in charge of air and water problems in the mine. It was explicitly directed that "he will not be in charge of a production gang." Spiedman's interaction with the line workers was also inhibited by the agreement that he would now work through top management in the plant. It is noteworthy that these two supervisors both epitomized certain tension-provoking characteristics.

Both of these men exemplified the use of "close supervision," and both of them had relatively few friendly, and informal, contacts with line workers. The delimitation of authority brought about by the memorandum of agreement withdrew their "line" powers, thereby segregating them from the production workers whose indulgency expectations they were continually outraging. As one worker explained the agreement ending the strike, "Ferdinand takes care of the foul air and lighting. He's not handling *men* any longer, so we don't care if he's a foreman or supervisor, *so long as he don't have to handle men.*"

The specification of authority provided for by the memorandum thus had the following results:

1. It reduced the rate of interaction between supervisors who used close supervision and the line workers. It reduced the rate of interaction between supervisors and line workers who had comparatively strained or loose informal ties.

2. In effect, then, it segregated supervisors and workers who did not share complementary expectations of each other's role.

3. It thus contained or circumscribed conflicts which might otherwise arise, thereby enabling more "peaceful" cooperation to take place across status lines.

In short, the increased use of bureaucratic administration served to reduce conflicts between different echelons, and functioned in this way as a tension-reducing mechanism.

There were other ways, also, in which the strike settlement served to reduce the conflict potential. For example, the new rules specified that union stewards must first receive the consent of their foremen before leaving their department, while another rule was to be established governing the conditions under which foremen might work. Both of these rules would serve to make explicit the discretionary limits of those involved. In short, the rules clarified rights and obligations, spelling them out and making them unambiguous.

It was hoped that, in this way, tensions arising, for example, from conflicting interpretations of the contract made by workers and management, and expressed in the "working foremen" grievance, would thereby be remedied. Actually, however, careful specification of foremen's rights does not entirely resolve the question of "working foremen," since, as we have seen, this grievance was in great part a masked expression of hostility toward closer supervision.

While the enactment of these rules does not reduce tensions springing from close supervision as such, it does, nevertheless, provide more firmly established yardsticks in terms of which a complaint may be handled. By establishing a more definitive basis for passing upon such grievances, the rules facilitate decisions concerning their remedy and disposition. Thus the extension of rules eases the decision-making process, somewhat reducing the role of procrastination as a conflict creating element. More generally, by removing or lessening the chances for a "misunderstanding" of existent agreements, the extension of rules may mend shortcircuited communication channels, and in that way reduce tensions.

If the use of bureaucratic mechanisms contains or reduces overt conflict, it is not, however, a "peace at any cost" mechanism. Indeed, it may be suggested, it reduces present conflicts in ways that *increase* the parties' ability to undertake *future* conflicts more successfully. The curtailment of Spiedman's powers, and the limitations of the stewards' mobility in the plant, both reduced the possibility that the "*junior*" officers of either group, union or management, might commit their respective sides to a conflict *without the consent of their supreme commanders.*

The new rules reinforced the decision-making powers of the supreme authorities in each camp by lessening the likelihood that those *down below* could make decisions which would result in *unanticipated* conflict. Under the terms of the strike settlement, the full time union functionaries agreed to allow the stewards to come under greater control of their foremen. Conversely, Lakeport management consented to delimit the powers of Spiedman and Ferdinand. The power of the union and Company both was now more centralized and it was less likely that the workers could once again act as an independent "third force."

What had been inhibited by increased bureaucratization, then, was not merely conflict, but unanticipated conflict, conflict born of low-ranking initiative and commitments. What had been reinforced was not merely cooperation, but cooperation in greater conformity with high level directives and plans. It does *not* seem adequate to conclude, therefore, that bureaucratization was adopted to reduce the tensions of the plant as a whole, nor merely because this pattern of administration aided in realizing the enterprise's formal goals, more production and profits. Instead, it was adopted because it safeguarded the specific *status*-interests of the Company and union leadership, enabling them also to realize their "private" goals, the maintenance of status prerogatives.[2]

---

[2] It is obvious that the formal union leadership on the local level, particularly Byta's clique, lost status in consequence of the strike. This, however, was also true for the union leaders above them, the national union's regional representatives. For the national headquarters would view a wildcat strike as evidence that these men had lost control over the local situation.

It is in part for this reason that certain of the tensions which underlay the wildcat strike were not actually reduced by the terms of the strike settlement. For example, the procrastination of the plant manager, leading to the breakdown of the grievance machinery and to workers' complaints about the "pile up" of grievances, stemmed partly from the managerial distinction between "complaints" and "grievances." Since a "complaint" was a worker's claim that infringed upon what management thought of as its prerogatives, and since the distinction as a whole was a way of safeguarding management's position, nothing was done to modify this tension-provoking aspect of the situation. Indeed, each of the solutions adopted may further intensify some of the tensions which originally elicited them. For example, the increased centralization of authority which was brought about, in order to keep the "hotheads" in line, may lengthen lines of communication and the time needed to secure remedies of the workers' grievances. The emphasis on modifying the use of the machines, running certain of them more slowly, neglects the fact that workers' complaints about the "speed up" were often only symptomatic of their hostility at the accompanying changes in the pattern of *supervision.*

Similarly, workers were not hostile to Spiedman merely because he "overstepped his bounds" or "cussed them out," but because he did so without being integrated in their informal system. Removing Spiedman, or Ferdinand for that matter, from interaction with line workers does not necessarily remedy the conditions which impair relations between any type of supervisor and workers. For the workers would tend to withdraw from friendly sociabilities with any supervisor who practiced "close supervision." Similarly, a "traveling" engineer who is unintegrated in the plant's social organization will continue to face the problem of getting his work done without access to the informal social system.

Management tended to expect that tensions arose when supervisors got "too close" to the workers. Their solution, therefore, was to remove supervisors from the situation. Management's tendency to define "closeness," in the sense of friendliness between workers and supervisors, as a source of tension derived in part from their desire to guarantee the "loyalty" of their supervisory staff, and to keep them responsive to directives from above. But it was precisely because certain supervisors, Spiedman, Ferdinand, the successors and strategic replacements, were insufficiently responsive to the *workers'* expectations and *overly* responsive to management's efficiency drive, that tensions arose between them and the workers. This situation was not repaired, if anything it was worsened, by heightening the centralization of managerial authority.

In fine, the participants did not respond simply to the needs of the "organization as a *whole*," but to those threats which impinged upon their *status* privileges, and in those ways which safeguarded these privileges. It is, in part, for this reason that certain of the organizational conditions which created disruptive tensions were not eliminated by the increased use of bureaucratic methods. At best, these were an administrative aspirin; they relieved management's "headache" temporarily, but since they did not come to grips with the underlying tensions, they could not effect a cure.

Chapter Nine

RUDIMENTS OF A GENERAL THEORY OF GROUP TENSIONS

UP TO THIS POINT, our task was the description of a unique industrial conflict, a wildcat strike. Hopefully, the analysis of this strike sheds some light on the events that occurred in the Oscar Center plant, and contributes, generally, to an understanding of strikes and wildcat strikes. In this section, however, these events will be divorced from their unique industrial setting, as much as possible, and will be examined in the broadest possible context—that is, in the framework of a general theory of group tensions.

A wildcat strike is a distinctive type of a social tension. Yet, in analyzing this strike, we were compelled, as any social scientist would be, to employ certain general assumptions concerning the manner in which human beings behave under tension. Many of these assumptions are applicable to the study of almost any kind of social tension. What will be done here, then, is to make these broad, latent assumptions manifest, and to codify them. In this form, they will be more readily susceptible both to critical inspection and to cumulative development. It is in this sense that our objective is to outline a general theory of group tensions.

The title of this chapter warns that only the *rudiments* of such a general theory are to be essayed. This implies, first, that only those elements deemed basic to the theory will be presented here; the frills will have to come later. One of the reasons for this is that we have chosen to take more of a "pragmatic," and less of an "axiomatic," approach to the theory. That is, only those parts of the theory will be emphasized which have proved of value in analyzing our empirical data; little effort will be made to develop those parts of the theory which can be derived from logical inference alone.

Secondly, there is, in the reference to "rudiments," the implication that even these basics will be formulated in a deliberately crude manner, with little or no effort to define the central terms. Indeed, the "charm" of the proposed formulations will reside in their ready intelligibility to any educated layman. Their scientific value, however, will rest on the extent to which they can *unfreeze* the theory of group tensions. By requiring minimal commitments to a parochial conceptual apparatus, a framework may be erected that can shelter many theoretical mansions.

Finally, it must be stressed that, as this will be a theory of *group* rather than individual tensions, the focus will be on strains in social systems rather than those in personality systems. It is unnecessary to belabor the obvious point that the two are connected, and that there is no tangible gulf between personal and social disorganization. Assuredly, the characteristics of individuals in a group contribute to and express group tensions. In some way, too, the disturbances of the individuals who comprise the group reflect and contribute to the development of group tensions, as well as to the attempts which are made to cope with them. In focussing on group tensions, however, the individual's neuroses or character deformations are treated as a "given"; disciplined concentration is instead directed to the tensions in the *relationship* between individuals. To use a crude typographical metaphor, a theory of group tensions is concerned about a unit of at least two persons, "A"———"B," and particularly about the relationship, the ——— between them, and in what severs or unravels it.

Operations in the Analysis of Group Tensions

In the initial phases of a study of group tensions there are at least two key operations which can provide an opening wedge. The first of these is the description and analysis of "symptoms." As used here, a "symptom" is a complaint about something. Since men under stress verbalize their grievances, by examining them, the zones of disturbance may be tentatively identified.

A symptomatic complaint constitutes a statement of frustrated expectation. For example, the complaint about the speed-up expressed frustration of an expectation that speeds would not be continually varying; complaints about Spiedman's cursing reflected violated expectations that supervisors would not overtly express aggression and disrespect for the men. A symptom, in this sense, is thus quite similar to the notion of "presenting symptoms" used by doctors to refer to the patient's description of his own disturbances. For in the medical case, also, the symptomatic complaint refers to a departure from the patient's *expectations* concerning the manner in which his organism will operate.[1]

The examination of symptoms institutes a problem in which the generic question is always: Under what conditions is it possible for the aggrieved party's expectations to have been frustrated? This, in turn, directs investigation onto two parallel avenues. On one of these, the study concerns the *expectations* which have been violated. For example, workers' complaints about management's "broken promises" suggested that they expected to be able to trust and to be trusted by management. Indeed, this was a general complaint to the effect that management was not even conforming with expectations which it had deliberately given workers reason to believe they would respect. Again, the complaints about "working foremen" evidenced the workers' expectation that foremen should not engage directly in production activities, at least under certain conditions. In short, the examination of symptomatic complaints helps to locate the frustrated expectation, or enables the analyst to make an inference about it.

There is at least one important case in which this must be qualified. This is where the violated expectation is not viewed as legitimate by the complainant himself. As a result, he either suppresses, truncates, distorts, or disguises his expectation in some manner, or displaces his frustration onto some other area, and formulates it in terms of a legitimate expectation. This was illustrated in our discussion of the wage issue. In any event, if the analysis of the complaint is not confined to its general formulation, for example, "the foremen around here have been working too much," and instead, proceeds by examining concrete instances of the disagreeable behavior, it is possible to get clues concerning the expectations which have actually been violated.

---

[1] *Cf.*, Aubrey Lewis, "Health as a Social Concept," *British Journal of Sociology,* June, 1953, pp. 109-124.

For example, in discussing with a miner a specific case of a foreman working, his comments indicated that he did not really mind if his foreman *worked*, but only when the foreman did so in a manner which increased his control and power over the worker. Thus the complaint about "working foremen" was, in part, a masked grievance expressing resentment at the violation of the workers' expectation that there would be no "close supervision." The complaint was distorted, and its real content obscured, because this expectation was only dubiously legitimate.

Concurring with the investigators of the Western Electric plant, our own "interviewers found . . . that workers by themselves were not able to specify precisely the particular source of their dissatisfaction, but that if they were encouraged freely, the effect was not merely emotional relief, but also, in many instances, the revelation to the critical listener of the significance of the complaint.[2]

The second avenue of investigation explored during an analysis of symptoms involves the *conditions* which frustrate the complainant's expectations. Thus, analysis of the "working foremen" complaint suggests that it was a response to an *actual* increase of close supervision. This, of course, can elicit further problems; for example, what led to increased close supervision? This, too, created further interest in the role of succession, strategic replacements, deteriorating market conditions, and so forth.

In sum, the analysis of tensions requires study both of the expectations which have been frustrated, and the conditions frustrating them; and each of these may be commenced by the analysis of symptomatic complaints. Stated differently, analysis of symptoms may lead to hypotheses about things which the complainant is defending, the things which are threatening, and the specific defense which is being employed against the threat. I take it that this is analogous with the conception of medical symptoms advanced by William Alanson White, which he characterized as "the signs of . . . combat and largely, at least, directly or indirectly signs of the way in which the organism is resisting destruction and combatting death. Symptoms as such, then, instead of being symptoms of disease, using disease in the sense of an entity, and therefore bad and indicative of dissolution, need to be looked at as beneficient in essence, for they indicate how the organ-

---

[2] *Management and the Worker, op. cit.*, p. 269.

ism is trying to save itself from the inimical influence by which it is attacked." [3]

The working foremen symptom, for example, was indicative of the threat that close supervision posed for the workers' work-oriented, authority-deprecating conception of their factory role. It indicated, further, that one of the specific defenses used by the workers was a legalistic interpretation of the contract, which limited the conditions under which foremen might work.

Clearly, not all complaints have relevance to a theory of group tensions. Stated positively, only insofar as complaints do have bearing on the relationships among group members are they of interest here. Often, however, complaints are formulated in a way that obscures their implications for a system of interpersonal relationships. In general, complaints seem to be classifiable into two types, those referring to the behavior of some other persons, and those referring to some set of "conditions." For example, the complaints about "foremen working" or about the "cursing supervisor" are clearly of the first type; complaints about the "export order" or the "speed up" of the new machines focus, in contrast, on a set of depersonalized conditions.[4]

The circumstances leading to these diverse formulations of complaints need not be examined here. It is important, however, to note that complaints concerning "conditions" can often be restated in terms of their implications concerning some *person's behavior*. If the relevance of a complaint for a system of social relationships is to be clarified, this is what must be done. The analyst must say, with some distortion of the Bard, "the fault . . . is not in our stars, but in ourselves," and show how these fetishized "conditions" implicitly involve human behavior. For example, the complaint about the "export order" was important as a reminder to the Oscar Center workers that the workers in the Big City plant were out on strike, and was thus

---

[3] William A. White, *The Meaning of Disease,* The Williams and Wilkins Co., 1926, pp. 118-119.

[4] This distinction was first suggested to me by the work of one of my students. See, Raymond Hartell, *A Paradigm for the Study of Problems of the Social Level*; unpublished Master's Thesis, University of Buffalo, June, 1951.

a validation of their own criticisms of the Company management. Similarly, the complaint about the speed up expressed, among other things, grievances concerning concomitant changes in supervisory *behavior.*

In analyzing complaints it should not be assumed, of course, that they constitute a valid description of some state of affairs. The question of the truth of any complaint is not the important question to be addressed to it. This is, at best, an auxiliary, useful in interpreting the meaning of the complaint, that is, its bearing on a network of social interaction. The important question, then, is not whether the complaint is true or false, but what it means.

In concluding this discussion of symptoms, it need hardly be added that it should be viewed as a programmatic preview. There yet remains the hard work of codifying the operations involved in the analysis of complaints, a task which must be done before a theory of group tensions can attain to scientific maturity. Since there exist formal mechanisms for the expression and communication of complaints in factories, they are more evident and easily located in such a group. Complaints, however, exist in *any* group under stress; as an initial point of departure, they need to be identified and analyzed; in short, they need to be taken seriously.

The Identification of Key Statuses

A complaint is a grievance about someone's behavior verbalized by someone else. In what terms shall these persons be identified and characterized? Since the task is one of analyzing a social system, the biological or psychological attributes ascribed to people as individual organisms are beside the point. What is needed is an intrinsically social basis for viewing people, one which directly focusses on their *inter-relatedness.* For this purpose, the most suitable and elementary notion is that of "social status."

This term can first be clarified by illustrating it. Social status subsumes such notions as "father," "mother," "worker," "employer," "teacher," "student." Any one person can, of course, occupy a cluster of several such positions, being a "husband," "father," "worker," *and* "union official." Each of these terms refers to a social position occupied by a person within a group. The individual occupying such a position tends to behave in ways similar to others filling the same position, and differently from persons occupying different positions. Thus, within certain groups, "mothers" will be found cooking, taking care of the children, shopping, and cleaning the house; "fathers" will be found to be away from the home "working."

One reason for these behavioral consistencies is that a given position exposes the occupant to certain culturally prescribed demands which define his rights and obligations. For example, "fathers" are expected to support their families; in our society, such support is normally the "right" of the mother and children, and they expect the father to provide this for them. Usually, also, this is the father's "obligation" and he expects to provide this support. In a similar manner, the workers in the Oscar Center plant had a cluster of expectations concerning their rights and obligations as workers, which were partly summed up in the indulgency pattern. Note that social statuses always come in pairs; there is no such thing as a solitary, disconnected status. A man cannot be a "husband" unless he has a "wife"; in order to be a "teacher" one must have "students." Similarly, one cannot be an "employer" without having "employees"; there can be no "management" without "workers," and vice versa. Thus the notion of status does directly concern itself with social interrelationships. But it does not do so in a way that mystically obliterates the component human beings engaged in interaction. Borrowing from Talcott Parsons, we will refer to such a pair of statuses by the terms "Ego" and "Alter"; Ego refers to the status occupant from whose standpoint the relationship to the other status occupant, Alter, is looked at.

Thus far, status has been characterized as a cluster of expectations directed at the occupants of certain social positions. There is, at least, one other characteristic of a social status needing mention here. This is the differential power which inheres in any pair of statuses. Ego may be more powerful than Alter, or the other way around. By "power" I mean the ability of a status occupant, Ego, to satisfy expectations despite the resistance of Alter. In a preliminary statement such as this, there is no point in discriminating the different types or sources of power which may exist. It needs to be underscored, however, that statuses may differ from each other, not only in terms of the expectations their occupants are customarily obligated to fulfill, but also, in terms of their power. This is a point at which a general theory of group tensions must not blink, and which it must, somehow, systematically incorporate.

In sum, if the first basic rule in the analysis of group tensions is that the complaints have to be identified and analyzed, the second basic directive is that the system of statuses which may be occupied by group members must be charted and the culturally prescribed expectations normally directed at status occupants must be described.[5] The analysis of complaints then proceeds by relating them to the context of interrelationships and expectations implicated in the network of statuses. The charting of status networks, however, is not identical with a sociometric picture of "interpersonal" relations. In the study of status relationships, the unit under study is not the person as such, but the person only insofar as he is an occupant of a culturally defined social status. This means, of course, that in a given group it is often possible to identify one status which is occupied by many people. The number of statuses is not necessarily equivalent to the number of people in the group. This leaves open the possibility that the relationship between two reciprocal statuses, say workers and management, may be influenced by the lateral relations which people in the same status have with each other. Obviously, the existence of a status organization, such as a trade union, and the resultant relations between union officers and followers, materially affects the relation between workers and management.

Propositions in a Generalized Theory of Group Tensions

These operational preliminaries aside, a generalized theory of group tensions may now be attempted. Let us begin by committing ourselves to a common assumption which has been fruitfully formu-

---

[5] This is similar to one of the key research directives which Merton suggests for the functionally oriented field worker. Analyzing a social pattern, he writes, "involves a report of *who* is variously involved in the pattern of behavior. And the description of the participants (or on-lookers) is in *structural terms,* that is, in terms of locating these people in their inter-connected social statuses." Robert K. Merton, *Social Theory and Social Structure,* Free Press, 1949, p. 56.

lated by Talcott Parsons.[6] This assumption states that the degree of tension in the relations between any Ego and his Alter depends on the extent to which the behavior of each satisfies the expectations of the other. From this it follows that:

1. *The more the behavior of Ego and Alter fails to satisfy the other's expectations, the more tension will there be in their relationship.*

This proposition is central for the entire subsequent discussion, and it is crucial for an understanding of the analysis of the wildcat strike. For example, the workers' complaints about management's "broken promises" were, in part, a colloquial reference to management's failure to comply with a variety of the workers' expectations. Following both the first and second successions, the workers' indulgency expectations were continually violated, leading to complaints about increased close supervision, about foremen who did not leave you alone but liked to "throw their weight around," about the restrictions in the use of Company tools and material, and about the decline of the expected, friendly, informalities with foremen.

According to proposition one, the amount of tension will vary positively with the frequency with which a given expectation is frustrated, and with the number of expectations that are frustrated. Workers' references to the "pile up" of "broken promises" suggest that they were not entirely unaware of this quantitative aspect of the matter.

Proposition one is ambiguous on at least one point; it leaves open the possibility that expectations may be frustrated from opposite directions. That is, frustration can stem either from *under*fulfillment of expectations, as in the above examples, or from their *over*-fulfillment. An example of the latter, discussed in the first volume of this study,[7] involved Peele's succession. At that time, because of Peele's anxiety in his new position, and because of his desire to "make good"

---

[6] T. Parsons, *The Social System,* Free Press, 1951. Parsons' formulation has been somewhat modified in our subsequent statement of it.

[7] *Patterns of Industrial Bureaucracy, op. cit.* A homely example of this is the annoyance of a parent when his child is "overly polite," and conspicuously demonstrates his newly learned manners by thanking the waitress each time she lays a piece of silverware before him.

at his better job, he tended to overconform to the main office's expectations, in part leading people there to speak of his "nervousness," and to complain about his overdependence on them.

Alter's behavior can be thought of as providing varying degrees of satisfaction for Ego's expectations, as being more or less in conformity with them. It is only rarely that Alter's behavior will precisely satisfy Ego's expectations. From Ego's viewpoint, Alter's behavior is satisfactory when it falls within a range of permissible variation. When it falls on either side of this zone of accepted variation, it can then be spoken of as either under- or overfulfillment.[8] It is in this sense that the following is meant:

1.1. *The more that Ego and Alter underfulfill or overfulfill each other's expectations, the more tension will there be in their relationship.*

One of the reasons that proposition one is so important is that, if it is examined carefully, it is possible to infer from it a large number of specific factors which contribute to an increase in group tensions. In other words, if a low degree of tension in an Ego-Alter relationship exists when the behavior of each satisfies the other's expectations, it is then possible to ask, in turn, what are the necessary conditions enabling this to happen? That is, what must exist if Ego and Alter are each to satisfy the other's expectations? Knowing this, it can be inferred that in the *absence* of these prerequisite conditions tensions will be generated.

Vagueness of Expectation

In the period following Peele's succession, while the new machinery was being installed, workers were found to complain about the effect that the new machinery might have on their overtime pay; they feared its possible reduction. One of the disturbances in this situation was that the workers did not quite know what to expect when the new machinery would be installed. This was a tension induced, not by the machines as such, but by management's failure or inability

---

[8] *Cf.*, George Homans, *The Human Group*, Harcourt, Brace, and Co., 1950, p. 295.

to clarify their possible consequences for the workers. In part, then, it was a lack of clearly defined expectation which strained the relationship between workers and management in this instance. This suggests the following general proposition:

2. *Tensions will be minimal when there is "some" degree of clarity in the expectations which Ego and Alter have of each other; tensions will tend to increase in their relationship when these expectations are "insufficiently" clear, or "too vague."*

The cautious wording of this statement derives from the possibility that there may be no one-to-one relationship between the amount of tension and the degree of clarity of the mutual expectations. In other words, the amount of tension in an Ego-Alter relationship *will* be reduced with increases in the definiteness and clarity of their reciprocal expectations. At some point, however, an increase in the clarity of an expectation may no longer yield increments of stability to the relationship and may, in fact, begin to generate tensions.

For example, the workers complained when Peele's personnel manager, Digger, usurped the former's managerial initiative and demanded to know, "Who's boss here, anyhow?" Nonetheless, they also complained when a foreman made his superiority openly evident and put forth clear cut expectations of obedience. In brief, while it can be asserted that mutual expectations must have some degree of clarity, if the relationship is to be a stable one, no commitment need be made, however, to the precise amount of clarity which is required. For there exists the likelihood that some degree of vagueness may also contribute to social stability, under certain circumstances. Perhaps, however, all that needs to be remembered here, is that tensions increase between Ego and Alter to the extent that their mutual expectations are unclear, *other things being equal.*

The role of unclear expectations in inducing stresses was evident in many basic features of the worker-management relation. For example, it was never very clear just how "hard" management expected workers to work. Nor were workers' indulgency expectations clear as to the point at which foremen ceased to be "good guys" and began to be "slave drivers" engaging in close supervision. At least equally important, was the indulgency pattern's failure to make explicit the worker's *obedience* obligations; instead it dwelled upon and ratified the workers' *technological* obligations. In short, workers had clearer expectations about working than about obeying; it is an example of what Harry Stack Sullivan called "selective inattention."

Changing Expectations

Following the introduction of the new machines, when their speeds and operations were being experimented with, the workers' expectations were very confused and uncertain. As the new machines' potentialities were being explored, workers did not know what new operations they would be called upon to perform or what level of "alertness" they would be expected to maintain. Expressing this lack of clarity of management's expectations, particularly concerning the machine's speed, were the frequent changes made in its rate of operation. The workers resented this instability, complaining that they did not like to work in a place where things were always changing. Thus, inasmuch as the clarity of expectations in connected with their stability, the following seems plausible:

3. *Tensions in the relationship between Ego and Alter tend to increase with the increasing instability of, or change in, their mutual expectations.*

The Integration of Expectations

Each of the parties to a relationship has a *number* of expectations that he wants satisfied; but sometimes these diverse expectations are not smoothly integrated with each other. Deficient in integration, a situation may arise where the satisfaction of one of Ego's expectations results in the violation of another. Alter is thereby fixed on the horns of a dilemma; the more he conforms to one part of what Ego wants, the more he outrages the other part. Thus:

4. *Tensions increase in the relations between Ego and Alter if either, or both, has a set of expectations which are mutually inconsistent, so that the satisfaction of one expectation leads to a violation of the other.*

The tension between seniority and efficiency, as criteria of advancement, was a notable case in point. In the relationships between middle and top management, each expected that consideration would be given both to seniority and to efficiency. These two attributes, however, were not necessarily correlated in any one man. Thus, if a promotion was made in conformity with the efficiency criterion, it might violate the expectation that it should be given on the basis of seniority, and conversely. This same inconsistency was also discernable in the workings of the contractually required "bidding system," which used both seniority and efficiency criteria as a basis for promoting rank and file operatives.

Another example of the tensions arising from inconsistent expectations was observable in top management's mutually exclusive directives to plant management concerning the manner in which they should handle a "complaint," as distinguished from a "grievance." On the one hand, main office management expected that the plant manager would eschew legalistic methods, and would not reject a complaint, out of hand, simply because it was not dealt with in the contract. On the other hand, however, top management enjoined the plant manager to withhold official cognizance from complaints that were not contractually acknowledged, fearing gradual inroads into their managerial rights. As a result, the plant manager frequently would not know what the main office expected in a given case. He would then refer the complaint back to the main office, to the dissatisfaction of the executives there, who might complain of the manager's lack of initiative, and to the disgust of the workers, who were made to wait while the main office decided the question.

The Organization of Attention

Before either Ego or Alter can reliably satisfy the other's expectations they must be aware of them. Up to now, the emphasis has been placed upon the characteristics of the expectations, for example, whether they are clear, stable, and consistently integrated. If tensions are not to develop, however, these expectations must also be *perceived,* and perceived in certain ways. It may, therefore, be proposed that:

5. *Tensions increase in the relationship between Ego and Alter if either, or both, does not perceive or is not aware of the expectations of the other.*

Formulated in this way, there are obvious bridges between a theory of group tensions and a psychology of selective inattention and unconscious distortions. This proposition seems to refer to the kind of situation usually described as a "communications breakdown." An important example of this, discussed more fully in the earlier volume of this study,[9] was observed following Peele's succession to the managership. At that time, he was so intently concerned with the expectations of the main office, that he paid little attention to the expectations of his subordinates. When Peele became aware of the tensions in his relations with them, and sought to curry their favor, he found he had little contact and access to them, and that he could assess their expectations only with difficulty.

Expectations: Illegitimate and Non-Legitimate

Not only must the expectations of each party to a relationship be perceived, if their relationship is to be stable, but they must also be defined in certain ways. Specifically, they must view each other's expectations as *legitimate,* as morally justified in that situation. A specific expectation is defined as legitimate, or not, in terms of the participant's values; this is, therefore, one of the important bridges between a "cultural" analysis and a theory of group tensions. It has been suggested earlier that a given expectation may be viewed as legitimate, as illegitimate, or, as non-legitimate, which may be thought of as a twilight zone of indeterminacy between the former two. It may, therefore, be proposed that:

6. *Tensions increase in the relationship between Ego and Alter to the extent that either, or both, views the other's expectations as illegitimate or non-legitimate.*

The most important cluster of non-legitimate expectations was, of course, the indulgency pattern. Non-legitimate expectations generate instabilities partly because those who hold them may not press for their satisfaction with the kind of forceful conviction that commands attention and yields subsequent gratification. Indeed, they may, for a while, withhold complaints even when these expectations have not been satisfied, thus allowing resentments to accumulate. This seems to have been the case with the union clique organized under Byta, who failed to communicate forcefully to management the workers' grievances concerning the speed up of the new machines

[9] *Patterns of Industrial Bureaucracy, op. cit.*

and the firing of the old foremen. It was because they were ambivalent about these complaints, feeling them to be of doubtful legitimacy, that their relationship with the workers broke down, and they lost their leadership. Management, for its part, felt that the speed of the machines, and the appointment of supervisors, was their own concern and "none of the workers' business." In short, they felt that the workers' expectations about these were illegitimate and, therefore, did not comply with them.

Perception of Behavior

Stresses develop, not only when one party fails to correctly perceive the expectations of the other, but, also, when he does not perceive the other's *behavior* as conforming to his own expectations, or if he sees it as violating his expectations. Alter's behavior itself, may not actually deviate from Ego's expectations, yet Ego may perceive it in this way. Thus:

7. *Tensions will increase in the relationship between Ego and Alter to the extent that either, or both, perceive the other's behavior as failing to satisfy his expectations.*

One example of this occurred in connection with the demotion of the old foremen. The workers expected that management would "give them a reason" for the demotions, and complained that this had not been done. Actually, management had given a reason, indicating that these men were demoted because of their inability to control the situation and to maintain adequate levels of productivity. Not believing this, the workers failed to perceive this as a "reason," and were resentful. Again, both successors, Peele and Landman, looked upon the workers as failing in their role obligations even before they came to the plant and had seen for themselves. Instead, they accepted the main office's definition of the plant situation, which led them to prejudge the workers as "goldbricks."

The Desire for Approval

Human beings usually desire and seek the approval of their fellows and, in turn, this motive disposes them to satisfy the expectations of those to whom they are related. It is an open question, however, whether they desire approval from every specific other to whom they are related. Needs for approval need not be gratified in any particular relation into which the individual has entered, nor must this need be satisfied in all of them. In part, this problem bears upon the question of the individual's reference group, the group toward whom he orients himself, and whether or not this reference group coincides with the group in which he is actually a member. This suggests the following:

8. *Tensions increase in the relationship between Ego and Alter to the extent that either, or both, does not desire the approval of the other.*

8.1 *Tensions increase in the relationship between Ego and Alter to the extent that either, or both, prefer the approval of some third party more than they do the approval of each other.*

In its relations with the workers, plant management operated under conflicting directives that led them to be ambivalent about securing the workers' approval. On the one hand, they of course preferred their relationship with workers to involve a friendly respect, rather than hostile feelings. On the other hand, however, main office management cautioned supervisors not to get "too close" to or friendly with workers, claiming that, if they did so, workers would take advantage of their friendship.

Similarly, our Thematic Apperception data suggested that Byta's group was concerned about maintaining the approval of *powerful* authorities. This, in turn, appears to have detracted from their need for approval by the workers, and the latter had a difficult time in keeping Byta's group responsive to their own wishes.

Negative Transference

In some way, it is necessary to take account of the fact that the persons occupying a given status have usually had earlier and influential role playing experiences. These earlier experiences are significant in several ways. First, they may give rise to "negative transferences" or "parataxic distortions"; that is, Ego may come to look upon Alter *as if* he were the Alter of an *earlier* relationship. As a result, Ego does not correctly perceive the expectations that the present Alter actually has. Conceivably, for example, a worker may perceive a permissive and accepting employer as if he were his harsh, demanding father.

Such distortions also lead Ego to define his *own* role in ways that violate Alter's expectations. Thus, the earlier role playing experiences may disrupt present Ego-Alter relationships by intruding inappropriate expectations concerning either the role of the self or the other. These earlier experiences may also influence Ego to define Alter as a person whose *approval* he does not want. This suggests the following:

9. *Tensions will increase in the relationship between Ego and Alter to the extent that either, or both, of them perceives the other as some earlier person who was disliked.*

Examples of this are found in the period following the first succession, when the workers began to fear loss of their overtime pay, as a result of the improved machinery. At that time, they suddenly began to speak of the callous way in which they had been treated during the last depression, more than a decade earlier, and how their wages had then been ruthlessly cut. There was the strong suggestion that an "eidetic" or imaginary person was intervening in the present relationship between workers and management. In short, workers seemed to be conceiving of present management as if they were the same management of the depression period, and to have displaced the hostilities they felt toward the latter onto the current management.

Distrust

The above suggests that one of the ways in which parataxic distortions impair social relations is by generating distrust; though, needless to add, this is not the only way in which distrust is engendered. As it is used here, "distrust" refers to Ego's expectation that Alter does *not want* to, or will not, comply with his expectations. In other words, Ego sees Alter as able, but unwilling, to satisfy him. Distrust is a specific type of expectation conducive to tension because it disposes the distrustful person to perceive malice where none may be intended, and thus to behave defensively where no defense is required. Such defensiveness can, however, elicit the very behavior which Ego fearfully anticipates. In short, distrust acts as a "self-fulfilling prophecy" which, in Robert Merton's words, is a "false definition of the situation evoking a new behavior which makes the originally false conception come *true*. The specious validity of the self-fulfilling prophecy perpetuates a reign of error. For the prophet will cite the actual course of events as proof that he was right from the very beginning." [10] The following proposition may, therefore, be suggested:

10. *Tensions will increase in the relationship between Ego and Alter to the extent that either, or both, views the other with distrust.*

Following the second wave of strategic replacements, for example, the new foremen distrusted the workers, in part because they were new and unfamiliar to them. This acted as a self-fulfilling prophecy when, because they distrusted the workers' willingness to work, the new foremen engaged in close supervision, violating the workers' indulgency expectations, and leading the workers to behave in the very disgruntled and apathetic way that the foremen had expected.

Power Expectations

One problem requiring consideration is, how can a stable relationship be maintained in a power framework? More concretely, what is the effect of the differences in power between Ego and Alter on the stability of their relationship? It would seem that similarities in the power of Ego and Alter should stabilize their relationship since, in this situation, neither can get what he wants except by satisfying the other's expectations. Contrariwise, the existence of notable power disparities makes it possible for the stronger to violate the weaker's expectations with comparative ease, and with relative impunity to his own satisfactions. Power would seem to make this possible, but not necessary. Thus, it may be proposed that:

11. *Tensions will increase in the relationship between Ego and Alter to the degree that there are power differentials between them.*

Like the other propositions, this, too, is "all other things equal." For if *similarities* in power are not legitimate, they, too, may induce tensions. This needs to be made perfectly clear; we are not

---

[10] Robert K. Merton, *Social Theory and Social Structure, op. cit.*, p. 181.

merely saying that illegitimate power differences produce tensions, for this is already implied by earlier propositions. We are saying, that, other things being held equal, the larger the power differential of any kind, legitimate or illegitimate, the greater the possibility of tensions arising.

This is so pervasive a phenomenon that it is often difficult to see. Consider, however, the comparative ease with which Peele made a great variety of changes after his succession; changes which were made in disregard, and in violation, of the workers' indulgency pattern. No comparable set of changes, with their concomitant tensions, could have been made by any ordinary worker. Consider further, that there was relatively little that the workers could do to obtain redress for their grievances and, indeed, the full expression of their resentment at these cumulating changes was held off for three years. Notice, too, that these changes began to be made when the power situation had been tipped in favor of management by the deterioration of the job market.

Deferred Gratification

The problem of power differentiatials in part expresses itself as a difference in the ability to defer gratifications. The party with greater power can usually wait longer to secure his satisfactions, nor need he satisfy the other's expectations until he is ready. The party with the lesser ability to defer gratifications may have to capitulate, and satisfy the stronger party's expectations, even though he does not consider them legitimate. This, of course, builds an enduring source of dissatisfaction into their subsequent relationship. It should be stressed, however, that an ability to defer gratifications is not only based on power, but is also a function of the previously developed *character structure* which the person brings into his role. These considerations then suggest that:

12. *Tensions will increase in the relations between Ego and Alter to the extent that either can defer gratification of his expectations more than the other.*[11]

---

[11] The problem of deferred gratifications was first called to my attention by research on "red tape," in which we suggested that an inability to defer gratifications was probably a character trait of those

As the work of Louis Schneider[12] and others has suggested, it is probable that middle class people are more habituated to the deferment of gratification than are workers (e.g., they "save for a rainy day"), thus highlighting the significance of the deferred gratification pattern for worker-management relations in particular.

CULTURAL CONCEPTIONS OF TIME

The ability to "wait" for the satisfaction of one's expectations is not only a function of the participant's power position or his character structure. It is also influenced by his culturally internalized conceptions of time, and of how long a "long time" is. For example, we have some expectations of how long it *should* take a letter to get to the person we sent it to; or of how long it should take a store clerk to bring what we have ordered. Indeed, much of the problem of "red tape" stems from the violation of expectations bearing on the time of performance. Thus:

13. *Tensions will increase in the relations between Ego and Alter to the extent that either or both fails to satisfy the other's expectations within an expected time interval.*

This seems to have been an important source of the workers' complaints about their inability to get a definite "yes" or "no" from management, and about the "long time" it took to get their grievances processed. More generally, our references to the work of Homans and Scott, with its emphasis on the role of the "run around," suggest that the frustration of shared time expectancies plays a pervasive part in the development of wildcat strikes.

---

[12] Schneider, *Ibid.*

---

who perceived a high incidence of red tape. See Alvin W. Gouldner, "Red Tape as a Social Problem," in Robert K. Merton, *et al.,* (editors), *Reader in Bureaucracy,* Free Press, 1952, p. 415. *Cf.,* the pithy account by Louis Schneider and Sverre Lysgaard, "The Deferred Gratification Pattern," *American Sociological Review,* April, 1953, pp. 142-148, for a systematic discussion. This work is a particularly valuable formulation of the deferred gratification pattern because the authors clearly see its implications for a theory of group tensions or, in Schneider's words, the problem of "order."

On Constraints

There is another and very difficult problem to which we must face up. It is revealed when someone asks a question like this: "It's all very well to say that a social relationship is stable when each person knows the other's expectations, when he considers these legitimate, and is motivated to conform to them. But this omits at least one important factor, namely, the person's *ability* to conform to another's expectations. Good will isn't enough; he must have the wherewithal."

Even if the notion of "ability" is somewhat vague, it is obvious that the question does bracket an important issue. One way of talking about the "ability" to satisfy someone's expectations is to conceive of it as a "constraint" which impels the actors one way or another. In other words, there may be constraints which forbid or prevent Ego from satisfying Alter's expectations; but there are also constraints which compel him to do so. For example, in the above discussion, we suggested that similarities in power between Ego and Alter constrain each to *satisfy* the other's expectations, and that when there are sharp power differences, the stronger may constrain the weaker to satisfy his expectations without granting reciprocal satisfactions. Here, however, we are primarily interested in constraints *forestalling* Ego's satisfaction of Alter's expectations, and inhibiting Ego's motivation to comply with them.

When a person says he is "unable" to do something, what he seems to be doing is to take certain of the circumstances in which he is involved and treat them as "givens" or unchangeable. At certain times, these circumstances may, indeed, be unchangeable; often as not, however, they are unchangeable only because the person has not thought of changing them or because he would not want to do so, even if he could. In short, commitments generate constraints.

Consider, for example, the man who says, "I'd like to get my wife that new coat, she certainly is entitled to it, but I am simply 'unable' to do so, since we're so short of money at this time." Here Ego's financial position is "constraining" him from satisfying Alter's legitimate expectations. Nevertheless, there are ways in which Ego *might* get more money than he has available; he might take on an extra job; or borrow the money; or sell some household goods; or even steal it. Ego's monetary position isn't actually so unchangeable in this instance, but he treats it as such. Why?

Generally, the reason seems to be that Ego would be more disturbed at exercising these options than he would at denying his wife's expectations. Perhaps this can be generalized and we can say that a constraint exists when a given pattern of behavior generates tensions for Ego. Ego, therefore, will be "unable" to satisfy Alter's expectancies when doing so creates more tension for him than not doing so. The underlying assumption here is that people tend to use options which minimize tensions, but this, of course, is assumed throughout.

A variety of different types of constraints can be detected; for example, physical, biological, psychological, status, structural, and cultural constraints. Examples of "physical" constraints can be seen in the working rooms of the miners, which are usually darker than those on the surface, not as easily connected with each other, and distantly located from the supervisor's quarters. The head of the mine might, for example, desire to be as exacting a supervisor as his peers on the surface, yet these circumstances make it more difficult for him to do so. Again, the men at the beginning of the board machine have expectations of sociable informal relations with each other, and would like to be friendly; but due to the way in which the machine is arranged they are frequently screened from each others' view and are "unable" to communicate. Here "unable" can mean only that it is easier to be silent than to talk to each other and that, therefore, it is more *probable* that they will be silent and less friendly than the other workers.

"Biological" constraints refer to certain mundane liabilities of the human organism; for example, its susceptibility to injury, illness, or death. Thus the worker says, "I was 'unable' to get to work this morning because I was too ill." Obviously, all he means is that he preferred not to be carried to work, and that he preferred the ministrations he would receive at home to those he would get in the factory! Again, the death of Old Doug constrained main office management to appoint a successor. His death, however, was a "constraint" in the sense that it would have cost management more to leave his post vacant, than to appoint a successor.

Personality constraints refer to the fact that people have certain kinds of developed character traits, attitudes, or personalities, which may make it easier or harder to fulfill other's expectations. Thus *one* of the reasons that Peele behaved in the rather impersonal way in which he did after his succession, thus dissatisfying the workers, was because his was a somewhat "cold," "rigid," or "shy" personality.

By "status constraints," are meant those conditions of behavior stemming from a social status that are taken as given, or unchangeable. Our initial reference to money as a constraint illustrates this type. In the case at hand, management's financial position was a constraint against the use of generous wage inducements which might have partially satisfied workers' expectations that they were entitled to "more money."

A "structural constraint" refers to those *social relations* which are taken for granted, and which dispose Ego to violate Alter's expectations. Thus, in the above case, management might have encountered criticism from the stockholders had they voluntarily offered the workers a large wage increase. In a sense, to risk such criticism is "impossible," for the tensions it may create for management are so much greater than the tensions aroused by failing to satisfy the workers' wage expectations. More generally, plant management might like to conform to their subordinates' expectations were they not similarly "constrained" by their realtionships with their own main office superiors.

Finally, "cultural constraints" are similar to all those mentioned above; they refer to things which are "unthinkable," not merely "impossible"; they involve an orientation to cultural norms which are taken for granted and the violation of which would create more tension than would conformance to them. Thus the man in the first example, could have stolen the money but only at more "cost" to himself than dissatisfying his wife. We have already noted, in an earlier statement, that tensions arise when expectations are viewed as illegitimate, because they then go unfulfilled. Here, the point is that an expectation defined as *legitimate* will tend to go unsatisfied by Ego if he can satisfy it only by violating some *other* expectation which he, Ego, considers equally legitimate.

It therefore seems possible to propose that:

14. *Tensions in the relationship between Ego and Alter will increase when the fulfillment of Alter's expectations generates tensions for Ego; that is, when Ego is "unable" to fulfill Alter's expectations.*

THE SANCTIONING RESPONSE

Is is now apparent that a surprisingly complex set of conditions must exist before Ego can satisfy Alter's expectations. In order for the relationship between Ego and Alter to be stable, however, at least one other major condition must be met even *after* Ego has satisfied Alter's expectations. That is, Alter must respond in a positively sanctioning way; Alter must express approval or affection toward Ego, he must "recognize" Ego's conformity in some appropriately rewarding way. In part, this is so because Alter's response serves as a security-giving cue, signifying that Ego is on the "right track." Thus:

15. *Tensions will increase in the relation between Ego and Alter to the extent that either or both fails to give a positive sanctioning response when the other conforms to his expectations.*

A notable case of this occurred when management replaced the old foremen, since workers believed that seniority should be rewarded. All of these foremen had also displayed their special loyalty to the Company by rejecting the allurements of higher paying defense plants during the war, and had kept working at the Oscar Center Plant. On this double count, then, the Company had failed to give a positively sanctioning response to men who were held to have earned it.

It should not be supposed, however, that the relationship between Ego and Alter is enhanced when Ego deliberately satisfies Alter's expectations in calculated anticipation that this will extract a positive sanction from Alter. At any rate, such a relationship is not as stable as one in which each views the other's expectations as his own obligations, thus as ends in themselves, rather than merely as a means of extracting the other's beneficence. For in the latter case, Ego's satisfaction of Alter's expectations is less reliable, and is more likely to take place only on the condition that Alter is around to watch Ego's performance and thus be motivated to reward him. "Close supervision" incites exactly such a response; the worker produces well only when the foreman is able to watch him, but "goofs off" when the foreman "turns his back." Of course, the foremen realize this, and watch still more closely; but they cannot watch everyone at once. Thus:

16. *Tensions will increase in the relationship between Ego and Alter to the extent that either or both conforms to the other's expectations only with the intention of receiving a positive sanctioning response.*

DEFENSE MECHANISMS

Assuming that Ego and Alter fail to satisfy each other's expectations, the resultant tension is dependent upon at least one other important element, the operation of "defense mechanisms." We assume that increases in tension may generate, more or less quickly and effectively, responses which serve to diminish the tension, that is, defense mechanisms. It would be sociologically naive, however, to assume that these defense mechanisms automatically and invariably develop in response to tensions, or that they do so with speed sufficient to cope with the tension before it gets out of hand, and that they always do so effectively. The point, however, is that when defense mechanisms do operate effectively the tensions are reduced. The development of tensions is, therefore, a function of the defense mechanisms. Thus:

17. *Tensions will increase in the relationship between Ego and Alter to the extent that established defense mechanisms are impaired, or to the extent that effective new ones are not devised.*

I take it that this is congruent with Robert Merton's observation that "The key concept bridging the gap between statics and dynamics in functional theory is that of strain, tension, contradiction, or discrepancy between the component elements of social and cultural structure. Such strains may be dysfunctional for the social system in its then existing form; they may also be instrumental in leading to changes in that system. In any case, they exert pressure for change. *When social mechanisms for controlling them are operating effectively* [*i.e., what we have called 'defense mechanism'—a.w.g.*] *these strains are kept within such bounds as to limit change of the social structure.*" [13] [our emphasis—a.w.g.]

One of the factors contributing to the wildcat strike, for example,

[13] Robert K. Merton, *op. cit.*, p. 116.

was the breakdown of the formally established grievance machinery which, in the past, had often served to reduce tensions. With the failure of this formal defense mechanism, tensions tended to accumulate. Similarly, when the supervisors' increased demands for "alertness" made it difficult for workers to continue using their former defense mechanism, namely, "withdrawal," this, too, contributed to the mounting tension in their relationship with management.

Tensions elicited by the inconsistent expectations of rewarding both "seniority" and "efficiency," were not resolved by the operation of what is, usually, a common defense mechanism in this case. That is, where there exist such inconsistent expectations, they are frequently mitigated by a defensive strategy which arranges them according to some system of priorities so that, in a given situation, one expectation is given clear precedence over the others. At least with respect to management's treatment of foremen, such a priority system did not develop.

On a lower level, however, with regard to the "bidding system" through which rank and file workers were promoted, the same tension between seniority and efficiency prevailed. Here, however, another defense mechanism, "conventionalization," had developed and somewhat reduced the strain. In the words of Willard Waller, "conventionalization arises when we agree to treat a thing as true whether it is true or not." [14] Thus it was pretended that *both* seniority and efficiency criteria were used to select men for promotion. Most everyone knew, however, that ability was practically impossible to use as a basis for drawing workable distinctions, and that seniority was, for all practical purposes, the sole standard employed.[15]

---

[14] Willard Waller, *The Family,* Dryden Press, 1938, p. 68. Waller is, of course, here using Sumner's notion of conventionalization; he seems, however, to have seen it in its dynamic and defensive capacity much more clearly than did Sumner. Surely this work by Waller, as well as his *Sociology of Teaching,* John Wiley, 1932, must soon be again "rediscovered," not merely as brilliant cases in applied or middle range sociology, but as among the most methodologically wise studies in group tension, made both from a functional and role-interaction viewpoint.

[15] For fuller treatment, see *Patterns of Industrial Bureaucracy.*

SUMMARY REMARKS

In the present chapter we have sought to codify certain assumptions concerning factors that contribute to increased tension in social systems. Obviously, there is a *great deal* more to be said concerning these conditions; there are a *great* many more propositions that can be formulated and need to be tested in subsequent work. If our codification has any value it is not as a finished task, but as another aid and stimulus to get on with the work. *Clearly, all of the propositions advanced must be understood in the "all other things equal" sense.*

In the next, and final, chapter we shall consider the kinds of "threats" which are inimical to the stability of social systems, drawing once more upon our own case materials. In addition, we will return to the question of "defenses," the response to the threat, and examine this more fully.

Chapter Ten

THREATS, DEFENSES, AND ORGANIZATIONAL CHARACTER

A GENERAL THEORY OF GROUP TENSIONS must develop some conception of the "threats" which disrupt social systems. It would be unwise, though, to fall into the "bacteriological error," that is, to conceive of threats as if they were insular entities, as external to the social system as germs are to the biological organism. Instead, threats should be thought of as both within and without the system, as an interactive blend of elements in the system and in the environment. Perhaps, therefore, it would be best to speak of "disorganization patterns," rather than threats.

The disorganization patterns discussed in the earlier chapters seem to congregate around two major foci: one of these is forms of social interrelations; the other is patterns of values, or shared definitions of the situation. Stated differently, we shall only concern ourselves here with the social and cultural aspects of "threats," omitting any analysis of their psychological components. In the first case, Ego and Alter need to be seen as part of a larger "social field" consisting of many Ego-Alter relations, and with each person having ties to a multiplicity of others. We must now surrender the assumption that Ego and Alter are a latter-day Robinson Crusoe and Friday on an isolated island.

In the second case, Ego and Alter can be thought of as involved in a larger system of values and beliefs which constitute a "cultural field." We must firmly eschew any implication that Ego and Alter have alone created the rules and expectations governing their interaction. Neither the social nor cultural field is, of course, separable, except for analytic purposes.

By labelling these two situations as "fields," we wish to stress that all the disorganizing influences are simultaneously present. They are not happenings in the past, but are processes in the present and incorporated in the things which people do, feel, and believe at this time. Nonetheless, these things are the *outcome* of certain "past" experiences and events. For some purposes, it becomes particularly significant to determine what these earlier experiences were. This is especially so, if they are "past" only in the sense that the specific Ego-Alter relation under study has already experienced them, but if they are *not* "past" for *other* Ego-Alter systems. From a clinical standpoint, knowledge of such past experiences is important, even if it does not aid therapy in a given case; for it may be invaluable for prophylaxis, enabling the clinician to prevent the emergence of disturbed states in others. This is one reason why clinical disciplines, in contrast with pure or analytic sciences, are concerned with "historical" or "genetic" development.

The following, then, are some of the disorganization patterns manifested in our case study, yet relevant in many other group settings.

PATTERNS OF DISORGANIZATION

(1) ROLE CONFLICTS AND CROSS-PRESSURES

Ego, of course, does not have relations with one Alter only, but with many. He does not occupy only one status, but several; these bring Ego into contact with a variety of people each of whom *may* place different demands upon him. It is, therefore, possible for one person to make demands on Ego which are contradicted by the demands of others. To the extent, then, that Ego is related to two or more Alters who place mutually inconsistent demands upon him, then his relations with one or the other, or perhaps both Alters, will undergo tension.[1] In these circumstances, Ego can satisfy the expec-

---

[1] A common case of this in industry is that of the union leader whose wife expects him to be home early, "like other men," but whose work demands that he meet with workers during evening hours. *Cf.*, Alvin W. Gouldner, "Attitudes of 'Progressive' Trade Union Leaders," in W. H. Kolb and L. Wilson (editors), *Sociological Analysis,* Harcourt, Brace, and Co., 1949.

tations of one Alter only by violating the expectations of the other. A typical case of this was the dilemma in which Byta's clique found itself. On the one hand, their formal position of union leadership oriented them to the workers' expectations that seniority norms would be respected; on the other hand, they were also oriented to the managerial emphasis on efficiency, as a prime basis for recruiting foremen, and to management's belief that supervisory recruitment was its prerogative. Byta attempted to resolve the consequent tensions by withdrawing from his official union role.

The familiar conception of the foreman as "the man in the middle" is an endemic case of conflicting role pressures. Here, the foreman's superiors expect him to deal with his subordinates in an impersonal manner conducive to efficiency. At the same time, however, the foreman has daily relations with workers who expect him to "play ball," and to conform to their time-worn informal practices, e.g., those involved in the "indulgency pattern."

The cross pressure situation which then emerges can be diagrammed in the following way:

The cross pressures situation, it will be seen, consists of two overlapping social systems, SS.1 and SS.2. Ego is implicated in both, and he is pulled in opposite directions by the conflicting expectations of Alter-1 and -2. The stress develops because of Ego's simultaneous participation in both systems, and because of the concurrent demands this joint membership places upon him. In short, neither System-1 nor System-2 is the "germ" creating the trouble. To the outside observer, if not to a participant, it is the joint interaction of the two systems that is mutually disruptive.

Going a step further, and asking, why is it that the expectations of Alters-1 and -2 were conflicting, it may be seen that they have both defined their situations in different ways, each being involved in different cultural systems (CS). This may be diagrammed as follows:

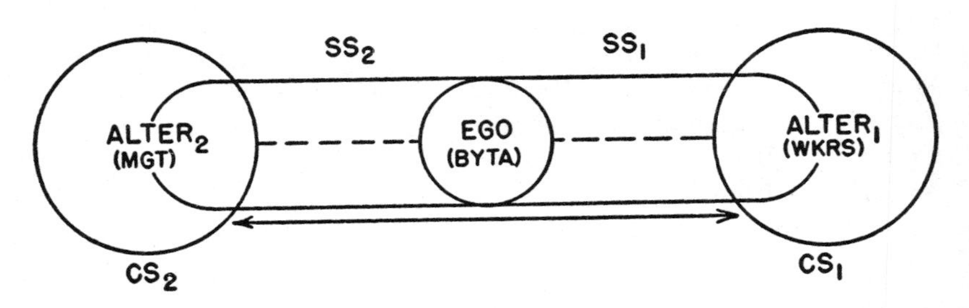

In Byta's (or Ego's) situation, the workers expected seniority to be rewarded, while management emphasized efficiency. The workers' seniority expectation was not an isolated conception, but was an integrated part of a larger cultural system, in which it was compatible. For example, seniority expectations were congenial to the "second chance" element in the indulgency pattern. Contrariwise, a stress on efficiency was not readily compatible with other parts of the indulgency pattern, such as "government jobs," "protection," or "no close supervision." In short, management's accent on efficiency was more compatible with cultural system-2 which stressed rational administration, i.e., taking no old practices for granted, constantly searching out new improvements, and focussing, not on the persons involved, but on the particular problem requiring solution.

(2) Authoritarian Administration

It is a simple but consequential fact that Ego's expectations may be more completely satisfied by one Alter than by another, and that one Alter may be capable of subjecting Ego's behavior to more powerful sanctions than another. This is part of what is involved in any system of administration, and is particularly true in an authoritarian system. In Burleigh Gardner's words, when "lines of authority converge toward the top of the structure, the lines of interest and attention converge too. In fact, everyone seems to be looking upward with his attention focussed upon the people above him and especially upon his boss. . . . While each boss is thus the center of attention from his subordinates, he in turn is busy watching his own boss and wondering about him. As a result he tends to look upon his subordinates in quite a different way. He rarely worries about their opinions of him. . . ."[2]

Generalizing on this, it may be ventured that relations between Ego and Alter will develop tensions to the extent that both are involved in an authoritarian structure in which Alter-1 is less powerful than Ego, and Ego is less powerful than some other Alter-2. One of the sources of tension in the Oscar Center plant was that there was a persisting tendency, as Gardner describes it, for people to seek the approval of those "above" them. In consequence, each attended less to their subordinates' expectations than to their superiors'. Foremen sought the approval of the building superintendent who sought the approval of the plant manager, while the latter, in turn, directed his attention to the expectations of the main office. The resultant disorganization pattern can be diagrammed in this way:

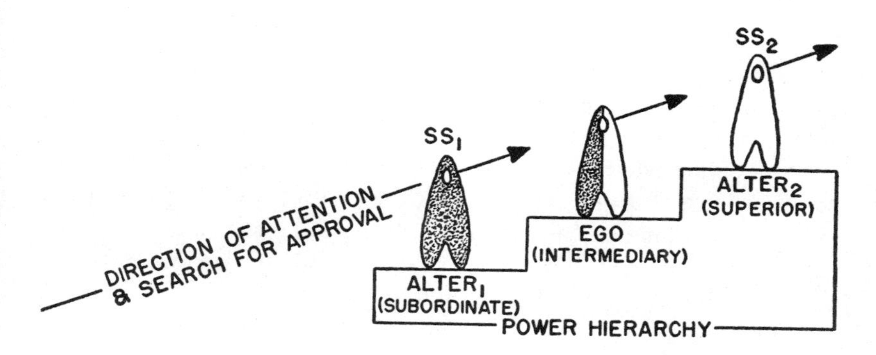

The distinctive feature of this pattern rests, not merely on Ego's greater power over Alter-1, but in the simultaneously greater power which Alter-2 has over Ego. As in the "cross pressures" situation, this pattern can be thought of as two interlocking social systems, SS.1 and SS.2. Here, however, it is conceivable that Ego *could* satisfy either of his Alters' expectations, without violating the other one's. Tensions arise because Ego is less apt to perceive Alter-1's expectations, or because he is less interested in securing his approval.

In this case, also, there are patterns of belief or ways of defining the situation which buttress the relationships, reinforcing the upward

---

[2] Burleigh B. Gardner, *Human Relations in Industry,* Richard D. Irwin, Inc., 1946, p. 9.

convergence of attention, and the search for approval from those above. For example, the common conception that management is "the brains" but that workers are merely "the hands" to do the dirty work, diminishes the respect and attention paid to subordinates, while intensifying that given supervisors.

Top management's ability to ignore certain "complaints," (as distinct from "grievances"), as well as middle management's often irksome caution in making decisions, seem dependent upon the existence of an authoritarian administrative system in the plant. More generally, the experimental studies initiated by Kurt Lewin, dealing with the effects of authoritarian group "atmospheres," indicate that such administrative arrangements induce more tension than democratic procedures, and lead, for example, to more aggression, apathy, and scapegoating by the subordinates.[3]

(3) Succession and Strategic Replacements

During this study two important sources of disorganization were focal, "succession," or the replacement of an individual occupying an executive status, and "strategic replacements," or the replacement of subordinate officers made by the successor following his own succession. Since strategic replacements are disruptive of social systems in much the same way as succession, being in a sense a case of multiple successions on subordinate echelons, both succession and strategic replacement can be discussed together.[4]

Following succession or strategic replacements, tensions may be induced for these and other reasons: A succession may inspire the successor either with fear or gratitude (and perhaps both) toward those who appointed him; that is, fear or gratitude depending, respectively, upon whether his new appointment was a demotion or promotion. The new man will, therefore, be often greatly concerned about his superiors' expectations and concomitantly, less responsive to his subordinates. This is a special case of disorganization induced by an authoritarian pattern of administration, as discussed above.

---

[3] Kurt Lewin, *Resolving Social Conflicts,* Harper and Brothers, edited by G. W. Lewin, 1948, pp. 71ff.

[4] Fuller discussion of these patterns is given in Chapters 3, 4, and 5 in *Patterns of Industrial Bureaucracy, op. cit.*

Secondly, by virtue of his newness in that particular role, a successor may not *know* what his new Alters expect of him, and, therefore, even if he wishes to, he may fail to satisfy their expectations. Thirdly, since the successor may have few friendly and informal contacts with his subordinates, he may not *trust* them to satisfy his own expectations, thus behaving in a prematurely defensive manner and generating a vicious cycle. In short, succession and strategic replacements induce tensions because they impair several, not merely one, of the conditions for a stable social system.

Underlying these tensions there are usually divergences in the values or cultural systems toward which the successor and his subordinates are oriented. Insofar as succession takes place as one expression of a larger drive toward rationalization, as was the case in this study, the salient values toward which the successor is oriented are rational, objective, and impersonal. If for no other reason than that the successor eagerly wants to show that *he* makes a difference in the situation, he is ready to try out new techniques and introduce changes. By contrast, however, his subordinates tend to remain committed to the older, traditional practices, which sanction informal deviations from the rules and acknowledge the force of established personal claims. Consequently, the successor and his Alters may be involved in differing cultural systems, with the result that each defines the other's expectations as illegitimate and is unwilling to satisfy them.

This disorganization pattern cannot be understood solely in terms of an elementary Ego-Alter system but must, like the others, be viewed as involving at least two interlocking systems with Ego, the successor, playing a part in each. The situation might be diagrammed in this way:

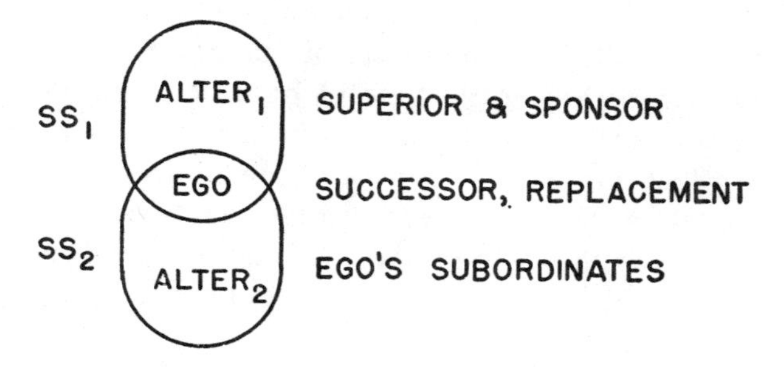

Several collateral points useful in the analysis of a succession might be mentioned here. First, the changes made in the state of SS.2 are initiated by Alter-1, a person often removed from direct interaction with the group affected. Secondly, and this is an easily neglected problem, note that some social system has been disrupted in order to obtain Ego as a replacement. Thus the need to replace one man can often generate a whole series of successions. In analyzing a succession, furthermore, attention should also be given the "predecessor," the man who formerly held the position, because reactions to the successor will be much influenced by what was thought of his predecessor. This is particularly true if a stable social situation had existed between the predecessor and his subordinates, so that he was well liked. Under these circumstances, there may emerge a "Rebecca Myth" which extols the predecessor, thus impeding acceptance of the successor. The disruptive potentialities of the predecessor remain, therefore, whether or not he continues as a part of the group or departs from it.

Another important component tension in the succession pattern involves the "old lieutenants" of the predecessor, the men who comprised his social circle and who were his closest assistants or intimates. The successor may fail to show the old lieutenants proper deference, willfully or through ignorance of their expectations, but in either event making them dissatisfied. This will dispose them to resist the successor and invoke the Rebecca Myth, and all the more so, as one of their own number had been conceived of as the "legitimate heir" to the position which the successor received.

Still another source of tension accompanying a succession is a pattern that may be termed the "legitimation crisis." The legitimacy of a successor is accepted if he has arrived at his new position in the "right way," and if, once there, he conforms to his Alters' expectations. It is noteworthy that the successor may fail to win legitimacy, on the first count, through no fault of his own. Thus the workers complained about the new foremen partly because they resented the manner in which the old foremen had been deposed. Furthermore, the workers often did not believe that the new foremen were any more efficient than those whom they had replaced, and they alleged that they had succeeded to their new positions by "underhanded methods."

Moreover, in the period immediately following the succession, there is a time of trials and "tests," in which the successor must, to some extent, validate in action his right to his status. Those around watch him, as they might any "stranger," to see whether he "measures up." They subject him to critical surveillance and restrain the expression of approval, before finally "counting him in." During this period, they may make exaggerated demands upon the successor, or lay social "booby traps" for him, while his flaws and failures are magnified by their concentrated attention. Unsure of his Alters' expectations and approval, the successor's mounting anxiety may drive him into behavior violating their expectations.

(4) TECHNOLOGICAL INNOVATIONS

Like succession and strategic replacements, technological innovation produced its disruptive effects not by any one of its consequences, but by the variety of unstabilizing agencies that it simultaneously activated. In the period following the installation of the new machines, when their optimum operation was not yet known, continual experimental variation in their operation induced uncertainties concerning managerial expectations.

Furthermore, a variety of changes in the workers' supervisory situation imperceptibly grew out of the technological changes. New technicians, such as Spiedman, entered the plant, and the workers were unfamiliar with their expectations or considerd them illegitimate. Similarly, the "brass" from the main office more frequently inspected the scene of activities and the workers did not feel free to behave in their customary manner. In effect, the worker-foreman relations had been disrupted by introducing people who were "powerful strangers"; that is, people whose expectations were difficult to gauge because they were strangers, but nonetheless important to know, because they were powerful.

Further compounding the effects of the new machinery, were what may be called its "fetishistic" consequences; that is, with attention directed to the changes in the huge mechanical props, the actors lost sight of each other. They focussed on their relation to the machinery, but neglected their interpersonal ties, creating a situation that may be called the problem of the "invisible Alter." This seems particularly true of management's behavior, responsible as it was for the innovations and for their successful application.

In large measure, the decisions giving rise to these disruptants were made by top management, and were passed down the line to be implemented by others. In effect, the decision was implemented by *reactivating* specific elements in the middle management's value system, elements which emphasized the desirability of rational and efficient administration. This rational component is usually under pressure by personal ties, friendships, and informal conveniences which have grown up; it comes, in time, to be suppressed in middle management's total outlook.

During a period of technological change, however, these submerged values are reaffirmed and restored to their salient position. In this way, managerial practices frustrating to the older, traditional, expectations are generated. However dormant rational, efficiency-centered values may become, they are always potential disruptants of comfortable tradition. In Emile Durkheim's phrase, "As soon as men are innoculated with the precept that their duty is to progress, it is harder to make them accept resignation. . . . The entire morality of progress and perfection is thus inseparable from a certain amount of anomy" or disorganization.[5]

(5) Market Pressures

Throughout this study it was suggested frequently that market pressures induced social instabilities. It was indicated, for example, that changes in internal plant relations were consequent upon changes in the plant's market environment. With the deterioration of the job and commodities market, management's power position within the plant improved, leading it to feel that it could "get away" with increased strictness. Another way of stating this, perhaps, is that management no longer needed, or was no longer quite so concerned with retaining the workers' approval.

Speaking of the market "environment" as disrupting the plant's social system should not evoke an image of the plant as floating in an amorphous, undifferentiated, environmental fluid. It should, rather, call to mind that management occupies a variety of social statuses, bringing it into contact with other Alters than the workers, specifically, competitors and buyers. In short, an "environment"

[5] Emile Durkheim, *Suicide,* John A. Spaulding and George Simpson (editors and translators), Free Press, 1951, p. 364.

can be thought of as *other* systems of Ego-Alter relations, connected with those at the center of study, but differing from them in that their behavior is taken as found and need not be accounted for. This might be pictured in the following way:

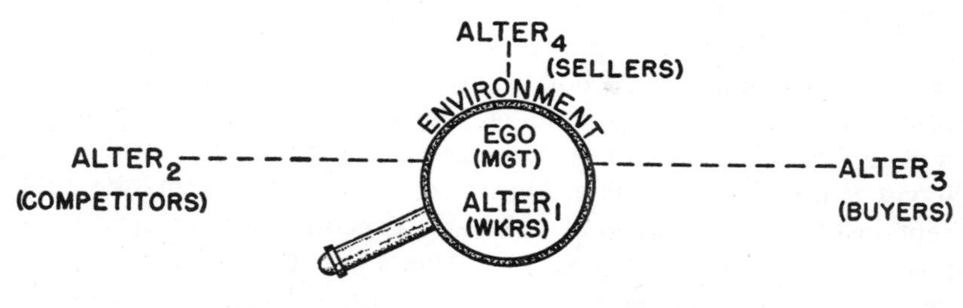

SOCIAL SYSTEM UNDER STUDY

Not only do market pressures contribute to sudden jolts in group stability, but they also provide a source of persistent tensions. These derive partly from the kinds of definitions of the situation ordinarily associated with market arrangements. Specifically, market institutions involve an assumption that the expectations of firmest legitimacy are those which have been given *explicit* consent. This induces stresses because any human relation, not excepting the contractual, always involves expectations which have *not* been mutually agreed upon in advance. As Durkheim argued, ". . . everything in the contract is not contractual. . . . But what shows better than anything else that contracts give rise to obligations which have not been contracted for [i.e., explicitly agreed upon—a.w.g.] is that they 'make obligatory not only what there is expressed in them, but also all consequences which equity, usage, or the law imputes from the nature of the obligation'." [6] "If we were linked only by the terms of our contract, as they were agreed upon," warns Durkheim, "only a precarious solidarity would result." [7] But there is another point here as well. It is this: market assumptions exert an unremitting pressure against the traditional, unstated, assumptions men inevitably employ, exposing

[6] Emile Durkheim, *The Division of Labor in Society,* tr. by George Simpson, Free Press, 1947, pp. 211-212.

[7] *Ibid.,* p. 214.

them to sudden challenges and unpredictable frustrations. In short, market or contractual arrangements do not generate instabilities merely because they fail to provide an adequate foundation of specific expectations, but also, because they actively corrode the other possible sources of stability. This is an important aspect of market functioning which may be termed the "explicit consent" disruptive.

Other market assumptions also impair the requirements for a stable social relationship. For example, conformance to the market postulate that "nothing should be taken for granted, but get it in writing," or *caveat emptor*, generates distrust, making it a permissible, if not a prescribed attitude toward certain Alters. Again, the conception of the *quid pro quo* stimulates expedient motivations, leading Ego to calculated appraisal of Alter's *quo* before he parts with his *quid*. Finally, market induced pressures to calculate consequences in advance, particularly in pecuniary terms, may impede transactions satisfying expectations, inhibiting performance within acceptable time intervals, and, also, leading to the neglect of expectations whose pecuniary implications cannot be calculated.

The Problem of the Labor Contract

Few social scientists have provided richer clues concerning the manner in which market and contractual mechanisms affect industrial stability than did John Commons. Commons noted, for example, that when the worker sold his labor to an employer he entered into an *authority* relationship; the economic transaction had political consequences. As Commons states, "What he sells when he sells his labor is his *willingness* to use his faculties to a purpose that has been pointed out to him. He sells his promise to obey commands." [8]

This seems legally true, at the very least, in the sense that, even in a union shop, a worker may be fired for insubordination. Commons' conception of the labor contract raises a number of questions important to an understanding of industrial tensions. For example: *Which* commands has the worker promised to obey? Are these com-

---

[8] John R. Commons, *The Legal Foundations of Capitalism*, Macmillan Co., 1932, p. 284. This is one of the masterpieces of American social science which deserves to be reclaimed from its premature obscurity and seriously drawn upon by industrial sociologists.

mands limited to the *production* of goods and services only? Under the terms of the contract, may an employer legitimately issue a command unnecessary for production? *Who* decides this anyhow, worker or employer?

That these questions bracket off real tensions, rather than academic surmises, is suggested by the Oscar Center workers' frequent complaints that they did not mind working when there was work to do, but they wanted to be left alone when there was none. It seems evident that the labor contract leaves unanswered many tension provoking issues centering around authority relations and work behavior.

Karl Marx's distinction between "labor" and "labor power" also converges on the same problem, but from a slightly different perspective. Marx stressed that the worker only sells his "labor power" to his employer, this being the *ability* to work; he does not, in Marx's view, actually sell a given amount of "labor" or real output. In his view, tensions arose when the employer attempted to transform labor-power into labor, since no bargain had been reached concerning the actual amount of work to be done.

Burleigh Gardner makes a similar point when he notes:

> Actually to the employer the labor he purchases is not a simple commodity such as a sheet of metal, which he can buy according to certain specifications as to size, weight, strength, and chemical composition, all of which can be tested beforehand, and which can be expected to remain stable. Labor as a commodity is even more perishable than a load of tomatoes, since it is the ability of a person to do work, and since this ability may vary from day to day and may be affected by all sorts of things.[9]

If the worker has sold only his ability to work, in exchange for his wages, how much of this ability shall be put into effect? How much shall the worker produce while under the employer's direction; how hard shall he work? These questions cannot be answered by inspecting the contract, for typically, this binds the worker only to a diffuse promise of obedience. In short, *the legitimate expectations of the parties to a labor contract, concerning both work and obedience, are unclear and vague, thus failing to provide a necessary condition of stability to the worker-management relationship.* The labor

[9] Burleigh B. Gardner, *op. cit.*, pp. 117-118.

contract may be well adapted to the shifting requirements of a changing *technology*; but, by failing to clarify the day-to-day expectations of labor and management, it contributes little to the requirements of a stable *social* system.

It thus becomes possible for workers and management to evaluate each other in terms of their own, unilaterally formulated conceptions of a "fair day's work," so that what workers conceive of as "fair" is viewed as "goldbricking" by management. Since obedience obligations are equally vague under the contract, it is also possible for workers to perceive managerial "diligence" as "acting superior" or "overstepping the bounds."

While workers have, in fact, legally committed themselves to *obedience* in entering a labor contract, we did not find them specifying their role in that way. Paralleling management's fetishism, workers also seemed to dwell on their technological role, on their production obligations, and gave these rather ready consent. But their relationship with people, their obligations of obedience in a system of authority, were especially ill-defined and vague. Indeed, it may be that the one-sided, but culturally pervasive, emphasis on the workers' technological function is implied by our very terms for factory roles. Common parlance has it that those on top of the industrial hierarchy are "bosses" or "managers," thus accenting their command functions; but those filling subordinate positions are spoken of as "workers," focussing on their technological responsibilities. In a culture which stresses equality, such semantic magic may have its function; but it is a service for which a price is paid in daily stresses and strains.

If a stable social relationship is one in which each party fulfills the expectations of the other, it is clear that the stability of the worker-management relationship does not rest firmly upon the contract. As Durkheim noted, other elements are required if the relationship is to be a stable one. In short, workers and management must derive their complementary expectations from sources other than the contract, from shared *traditional* beliefs and values. But if, on the one hand, the labor contract contributes little to a framework of clear expectations sustaining stable industrial relations, the "explicit consent" disruptant within it, on the other hand, makes vulnerable all the traditional supports that could lend such stability.

Furthermore, the question is not merely whether workers and management share a set of beliefs in *general*. The question is, do they share and utilize a set of common beliefs in their *particular* industrial situation? The extent of their adherence to a common set of beliefs, in this setting, could be overemphasized. For as has been seen throughout, many workers were oriented to the beliefs of the indulgency pattern, beliefs which were noticeably variant from the impersonal, efficiency-centered outlook distinctive of management.

(6) Paradigmatic Experiences

It is a commonplace among social scientists, that men perceive, judge, and react to current situations in terms of "frames of reference" derived from their past experiences. The notion of the frame of reference refers to those internalized standards which enable the person to assess and react to a stimulus. Karl Mannheim has proposed a collateral notion, that of the "paradigmatic experience," [10] which, as I interpret it, refers to the *specific* past experiences which group members have had, or think they have had, and in terms of which they respond to new experiences. These are not the unique experiences of any one person, but are *shared* experiences or shared conceptions of experience.

Nor is the paradigmatic experience a generalized, abstract value. It refers, instead, to a highly concrete, complex total situation in which values are implicated. The paradigmatic experience thus underlies and gives tangible definition to a general value, but it is not identical with it. For example, the spy in the motion picture "Five Fingers" may be said to have valued "money," or "wealth," and was thereby led into espionage. But money or wealth had specific connotations for him; money meant something quite different to him than it would have to another person who seemingly put a similar value on "money." To "Five Fingers," money meant the opportunity to become the poised gentleman he had once observed from a South American harbor, standing serenely on a penthouse terrace, immaculate in his crisp, linen jacket, and anticipating the exotic foods silently placed before him by soft-treading servants. "Money" was thus a congeries of tactile, kinaesthetic, visual, aural, and taste

---

[10] See Karl Mannheim, *Diagnosis of Our Time,* Oxford University Press, 1944. The following account is not intended as an exegesis of Mannheim's concept, but, instead, uses it as a point of departure.

images uniquely interwoven with social symbols. This cannot be summed up by saying, he put a value on "money," nor even on "all the things that money can buy."

In this case, the paradigmatic experience is a model to be consummated, or an experience to be recreated; it is the "good time" to be realized or lived anew. As such, it channels and directs behavior in the present. Conversely, however, a paradigmatic experience may be the "bad time" to be avoided again at all costs; this, too, influences the course of ongoing behavior. For example, there exists at least one American company, *not* the General Gypsum Company, which was sued in a governmental anti-trust action several decades ago. But to this day, and even though its personnel have almost completely changed since then, its executives have a keen fear of another such anti-trust action and bend their efforts to prevent its recurrence. Many of its current actions, particularly its energetic public relations program, are fundamentally aimed at obviating another such traumatic experience.

One of the most powerful paradigmatic experiences shared by many of the Oscar Center workers was the crisis of the last depression, and of others which had preceded it. Even the most superficial contact with older members of the working force clearly indicates that the experience of the 1930's is still very much of a potent force, a force easily neglected and underestimated in cross-sectional factory studies which ignore historical depth.

Paradigmatic *crises,* the bad times to be avoided but remembered, are related to group tensions in several ways. First, as we noted during the 1948 negotiations, the Oscar Center workers' references to management's depression behavior served to legitimate present hostilities. In effect, they justified present conflicts in terms of past indignities. Secondly, they evoke eidetic or imaginary persons, so that the current Alter is viewed as if he were the punishing or depriving Alter of earlier times, leading sometimes to prematurely defensive behavior, to incorrect perception of Alter's expectations, and to a distrust of Alter which may be unwarranted.

The relationship between the past paradigmatic crises and the present tensions is a two-way affair. On the one hand, the paradigmatic crisis may, in the above ways, *precipitate* tensions in a social relation. On the other hand, however, current *tensions can evoke the paradigmatic crisis* in whose terms the conflict may be made meaningful, legitimate, and which can strengthen the solidarity of those sharing the experience or believing in it.

(7) ROLE DISCONTINUITIES

The success with which Ego and Alter will perform their roles is partly dependent on the kind of earlier role-playing experiences which they have had. If their earlier roles have given them experiences in accepting and satisfying the role expectations now directed at them, the possibilities of Ego-Alter tensions are diminished. If, however, their earlier roles have developed expectations at variance with the demands that current roles place upon them, then tensions may be expected to mount. This hiatus is referred to as a "role discontinuity."

The most consequential, if commonplace, of such discontinuities were found between the earlier role playing experiences in the small communities, from which the workers came, and the factory roles which they now played. These communities were egalitarian in outlook; though they had systems of stratification, the common definition stressed the essential equality of neighbors. Factory roles, however, required that some give commands and others obey them. Though the authority system in the factory also tended to be blurred, its system of command was much more evident than that in the community. The plant manager, building superintendents, foremen, and workers were organized as a graded system of ranks visible to all. It would seem partly for this reason that workers chafed against "close supervision" and were hostile to "slave drivers." The experience of democratic community participation did not generate expectations congenial to the essentially authoritarian regimen of factory life.

Moreover, as a small community stressing the virtues of neighborliness, the relations of community members were predominantly informal and personal. A man was judged, at least in some part, by the family from which he had come. His public reputation was influenced by his parents', and their parents', past performances. It meant something to say, "Jim is the Anderson's boy." A man's idiosyncracies were known, his personal problems and family's needs were taken into account in dealing with him.

All this was not forgotten in the factory, and especially not by the workers, as the indulgency pattern suggests. Yet, the accent in human relations was placed differently. Relations tended to be more formal and official, for others outside the community had to be given an accounting. Whose boy you were no longer counted for so much; as Digger put it, "relatives don't cut any ice." A man made out, or he didn't, depending on his own performance. While it was difficult for a foreman to fire a worker if he knew his wife and children, still a man was expected to "keep on top of his job" or let someone else have it.

Thus there were important differences here; the community and the factory were divergent ways of life. Experience in the small community did not generate expectations that made for ready adaptation to the requirements of a modern industrial plant, and thereby provided a steady source of plant tensions.

The Analysis of Disorganization Patterns

In the foregoing, a number of disorganization patterns were singled out for brief discussion. By a disorganization pattern we mean some cluster of social relationships, or culturally induced conceptions of a situation, which impairs the requisites of a stable social system, as they were considered in the previous chapter. Among the disorganization patterns discussed were: "role conflicts"; "authoritarian administration"; "succession" and "strategic replacements" which involved the "legitimation crisis" and the "resistance of the old lieutenants"; "technological innovations," as a part of which were found the patterns of the "powerful stranger," "fetishism" or the problem of the invisible Alter, and the perfectionist strains induced by "rational values"; "paradigmatic crises"; "market pressures" partly involving the "explicit consent" disruptant; and, finally, "role discontinuities."

In selecting these disorganization patterns for attention, it is not implied, of course, that they were the only, or the only important forms of disruption. There are other important ones, certainly. In fact, a vital part of the cumulating analysis of group tensions consists of the identification of other patterns of social disorganization. If these, however, are to contribute to the development of a *general* theory of group tensions, the disorganization patterns must be characterized on a broad level of generality, permitting them to be discerned in many, varied group contexts.

It would seem possible, even in this preliminary formulation, to specify several operations useful in the analysis of disorganization patterns:

(1) In working with Ego and Alter as an interacting system, treat it as a system composed of interacting parts; do not focus on the system to the exclusion of the parts. This *caveat* is helpful in analyzing disorganization patterns since the pattern may arise on the unilateral initiative of either Ego or Alter, and not necessarily because of their mutual and simultaneous action. For example, the disrupting role of succession, strategic replacements, and technological innovations were obviously matters of managerial initiative. In short, identify those whose behavior within the system initiates the tensions.

(2) In analyzing pressures on the system from its "environment," notice that they need not impinge simultaneously on both Ego and Alter but may, instead, affect one of them first. Thus the disruption produced by the change in market forces first affected management; it was primarily through management's adjustment to this that its relations with workers came to be impaired. For a dynamic analysis of disorganization patterns, therefore, determine whether environmental pressures affect one of the parties before the others, and specify which one this is.

(3) In analyzing the disruptive stimuli emanating from the system's "environment," conceive of Ego and Alter as involved in a network of many other Ego-Alter systems, through which the disturbances are transmitted. Thus the plant's "market environment" can be conceived of in terms of the relationship between the management and its other Alters, such as competitors, buyers, or sellers. This involves three points: First, that a system's environment itself consists of Ego-Alter systems. Secondly, that Ego and Alter are articulated with these environing systems by virtue of the fact that each of them plays several roles, and not merely one. Third, and finally, that changes in a given Ego-Alter relationship may be brought about by changes in the other roles which each is performing.

Defenses

When the Ego-Alter system experiences disorganization, we assume that responses will tend to be made which reduce the resultant tensions; these responses to tensions are called "defenses." A great deal of the behavior described in our case history may be understood as "defensive," and it is one of the ongoing problems of developing research in this area to identify the recurrent patterns of defense utilized in social systems. As a corollary long range goal, it is especially desirable if further research can determine the specific defenses arising in response to different disorganization patterns.

For example, Roland Warren[11] has suggested that role conflicts may be coped with by a defensive segregation of roles, so that "not all cultural roles are activated at the same time by any one individual." Again, he proposes that role discontinuities may be responded to by "anticipatory training"; that is, by "early training in anticipation of future roles." A similar, but broader and more generalized, defense mechanism is suggested in Robert Merton's conception of "anticipatory socialization." This involves an identification with groups in which one is not yet a member, but in which one aspires to play a role, thus inducing the preparatory internalization of expectations involved in the later role. The parallel alignment of specific defenses and distinctive disorganization patterns has clinical value, in that, when a specific defense is observed, it could be treated as a "symptom," suggesting the particular patterns of disorganization underlying it.

In our own research, a great many defense mechanisms were detected, though no effort was made to correlate them with types of disorganization patterns. Some of these defense mechanisms seem to be peculiar to the particular industrial context of our research, while others can be stated in ways suggestive of their application to different group settings. For example, the "wildcat strike" itself may be viewed as an industrial defense mechanism which workers directed against management's use of "close supervision," and the consequent violation of the indulgency pattern. The same may be said of the emergence of the "wage issue."

Initially, close supervision gave rise to "withdrawal," either in the form of quitting the job or as expressed in "apathy"; this, too, was a defense mechanism, though one *not* peculiar to factory groups. Looking at the wildcat strike in a more general light, and in terms

---

[11] Roland Warren, "Social Disorganization and the Interrelationship of Cultural Roles," *The American Sociological Review,* February, 1949, pp. 83-87. This is a very cogent and suggestive preliminary codification of elements involved in a general theory of group tensions.

of its distinguishable component elements, there was a "circulation of leadership" from Byta to Izzaboss, which may also be regarded as a type of defense mechanism possible in many other situations and groups. The managerial distinction between "grievances" and "complaints," largely a distinction between "obligations" and "liberties," was a defense against the gradual violation of managerial prerogatives. Finally, though hardly exhausting the battery of visible defense mechanisms, there was the increased development of "bureaucracy" entailed by the strike settlement.

It is especially worthy of note that the defense of one party, say the workers, can create tensions for the other, management; obviously, for example, the workers' defensive wildcat strike was a threat to management. In other words, a defense mechanism is not merely a response to disorganization, but it may also *induce* a disorganization pattern. Any given pattern of behavior should not, therefore, be viewed as intrinsically either a defense mechanism or a disorganization pattern; a particular pattern of behavior might be both. Thus "strategic replacements" can, as indicated earlier, generate disorganization patterns; but it is, also, frequently a response to the tension experienced by a successor, being one of the ways in which he copes with the resistance of the old lieutenants.

Again, technological innovations were a defensive response to threatening market changes; but they were, in turn, also threatening to workers. Thus in analyzing either a threat or a defense, it must always be located in a specific Ego-Alter relationship. For example, the technological changes were a defensive response made by management to threats which it experienced in relations with specific Alters, competitors, sellers, etc. Viewed, however, in the context of management's relation with the workers, this same pattern of behavior was a threat. The notion that a threat in one Ego-Alter relation can be a defense in another might be diagrammed in the following way:

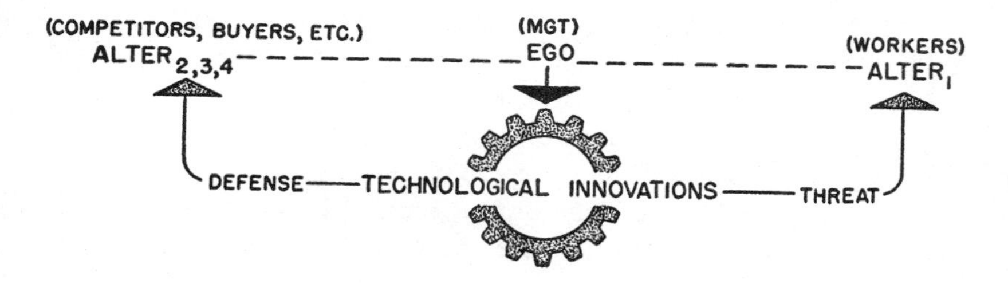

The Selection of Defenses

In studying defenses, it is a deceptive simplification to conceive of them merely as responses to disorganization. For, in leaving it at this, there is no basis for understanding why one rather than another pattern of defense is utilized. Instead, defenses have to be viewed as *selective* responses to threats. They are produced not only by the threat itself, but are selected and shaped by elements within the threatened system. In the next several paragraphs, we want to outline some of the elements influencing the selection of defense mechanisms.

One way of examining this question is to raise a key problem: *what* is the defense defending? First, it may be suggested that the defense is defending the *relationship* between Ego and Alter, and, by maintaining it, enables each to secure continued satisfactions. A defense such as "bureaucracy" appears to operate in this manner. It would be a grave error, though, to suppose that all defenses function in the same way. For example, insofar as "withdrawal," especially quitting the job, serves as a defense, it certainly does not result in the maintenance of that worker's relationship with that management; it clearly severs it. It is conceivable, however, that the withdrawal of certain intensely hostile persons might strengthen the relationship among those remaining, but this is debatable.

There is a second type of answer indicating what the defense is defending. It may be posited that another of the things being defended is to be found in the specific status occupied by Ego or Alter. In other words, defenses may be chosen in terms of their ability to safeguard status interests. At any rate, this heeds our earlier injunction that, in focussing on the system as an interacting unit, we should not lose sight of the interacting *parts*. For even if Ego and Alter have joint recourse to a single pattern of defense which serves to maintain their relationship, nevertheless, each of them may still be gaining something different from it.

For example, management's selection of the various forms of rationalization, namely, technological innovations, succession, and strategic replacements, cannot be understood solely as a response to threatening market conditions. For an alternative defense, heightening the workers' morale and willingness to produce, was largely neglected. The defenses chosen were uniformly characterized by their accessibility to managerial control, while the defense rejected might have made management dependent upon a resource on which it could not rely. More concretely, management preferred to forego joint labor-management determination of machine speeds, as one way of enhancing workers' morale and motivation, since this infringed upon what management conceived of as its status rights.

Similarly, the managerial distinction between "complaints" and "grievances" has, as we saw, all manner of *disturbing* effects upon the worker-management *relationship*. Yet management developed this distinction since it served to fortify those of its rights which it considered essential and proper for its status. In short, certain defenses were selected because they protected status positions, and, perhaps, especially, the differential advantages and opportunities involved in them. Ego and Alter choose defenses, then, not only in terms of their contribution to the system as a whole, but also because they defend their position in the relationship.

Another element influencing the selection of defense mechanisms are the values of those initiating the defense. Ego or Alter will prefer defenses which are legitimate in terms of their own values, and will tend to reject defenses they define as illegitimate. For example, the expression of aggression against supervisors by workers, a form of defense, was inhibited insofar as workers considered supervisors to be members of their own sociable, primary groups. When, however, the interaction between the new foremen and the workers declined, and when supervisors were no longer "counted in" as members of these primary groups, workers could permissibly express aggression toward them.

Again, when management violated the workers' indulgency pattern, the kind of defenses which workers could employ were affected by their conception of the indulgency pattern. That is, since workers did not view this pattern as having clear-cut legitimacy, they could not use formal, contractual mechanisms of defense against its violation. Instead of making public demands for contractual redress, they invoked the Rebecca Myth, staged guerrilla forays such as the wildcat strike, or displaced their resentment into a defense of firm legitimacy, like the wages issue.

Not only will considerations concerning the legitimacy of a defense affect its selection, but expedient considerations also play a role. For even though a given defense is deemed legitimate, it may, nonetheless, be rejected if it is judged to be ineffectual. When, for example, management began to "tighten the bit" and exert closer supervision of workers following the end of World War II, it did so because it believed that lax war time habits were improper, and, also, because "tightening up" was now *expedient* in view of the increasing scarcity of jobs.

Even if a defense is both legitimate and expedient, it still is not always possible to use it. For example, a defense needs to be congruent with the personality structure of those using it. In discussing the motivations of Byta's clique, it was noted that they typically derived much of their security from submission to authority, and that they ordinarily inhibited the expression of aggression. These men would, of course, find difficulty in using a wildcat strike as a way of defending themselves.

Another basis for the selection of defenses relates to the conceptions held about the causes of the tension. Not being automatons, the people involved will have some notion of the *causes* of the tension which they experience, however correct or incorrect it may be. They will respond, in short, in terms of their understanding of what brought it about. For example, insofar as certain workers, particularly those in Byta's group, believed that the strike was brought about by a "misunderstanding of the contract," supposedly made possible by its ambiguities, they favored the elaboration of bureaucratic rules to eliminate the areas of uncertainty. Again, management's conception that labor-management strife stemmed from "close" relations between foremen and workers, encouraged it to reduce tensions by getting rid of the offending foremen and putting in new and unfamiliar ones (strategic replacements), and by increasingly regulating their relations with workers by impersonal, bureaucratic rules.

Generally, there seemed to be at least three distinguishable conceptions which people in the plant had of tension-*causes*, the "naturalistic," the "utilitarian," and the "voluntaristic," each of which disposed them toward different patterns of defense. The "naturalistic" conception viewed tensions as rooted in the nature of things, perhaps in "human nature," and thus saw them as unremovable. For example, there was widespread violation of the "no smoking" rule in the plant. Since, however, smoking was widely viewed as an uncontrollable expression of "nervousness," few efforts were made to change the pattern. "Laisser-faire" is a response to a "naturalistic" conception of tension-causes. One of the prevalent conceptions of the strike approximated this. It maintained that the strike was a "spontaneous" eruption from below, and an expression of irrational feelings, to which a section of management responded by prescribing "catharsis," that is, allowing things to run their course, in the hope that this alone might remedy matters.

A "voluntaristic" conception of tension-causes attributes the difficulty to someone's *intention.* It does not view tension as the unanticipated consequence of certain activities, but as the deliberate end of the people involved. Such a definition of tension-causes frequently elicits punishing and aggressive responses. Thus the main office production department, in particular, viewed the strike as a deliberate strategem of the workers to enhance their control over the plant; they were then inclined to join battle with the aggressive expectation of "showing them who is boss."

In the "utilitarian" view, tensions are thought to be generated *accidentally,* being due, perhaps, to the *ignorance* of the people who bring them about rather than to their malice. A frequent defense against tension so conceived is to "educate" the offenders. This conception appears to underlie the Company's human relations program, with its use of motion picture strips and discussion sessions, providing some education in the difficulties of human relations.

Before the participants in a social system can have some conception of the causes of the tensions they are experiencing they must, of course, have some degree of *awareness* of the tension itself. The degree of awareness which they have of the tension will, further, affect their development of defenses against it. In the extreme case, for example, where there is little or no awareness, defenses can develop only in a groping trial and error manner, in an unthinkingly reflexive or habit-dominated way. Or defenses may be brought to bear on the tension only "too little and too late." This appears to be the case during the introduction of the new machines when, because management was attending to the technological problems these created, they neglected the dissatisfactions which had developed among the workers, permitting them to grow unchecked.

People also seem to use standardized "cues" which enable them to detect tensions. When they "see" these, even though they may perceive them without full awareness, their defenses against the tensions begin to be mobilized. For example, executives in the personnel department felt that when workers started complaining about "foremen working" something was wrong in labor-management relations, even if they did not know exactly what it was. Quite commonly, management uses demands for a wage increase as a clue to an impending or existing tension. Certain tensions may arise and remain unnoticed, however, where the participants have not developed cues signifying their presence. There did not, for example, seem to be any standardized cues, which management used at any rate, heralding the collapse of the formal union leadership.

To sum up this section: among the forces acting to select certain defenses, and to reject others, were the needs of the relationship among the parties involved, the status interests and pressures of these parties, their values, their judgments concerning the expedience of the defense, the psychological constraints acting upon them, their awareness of the tension, and the conception of the tension's causes.

ORGANIZATIONAL CHARACTER

In the analysis of defense maneuvers, there is at least one other problem of major importance, a problem which may be termed the "career of the defense." That is, the stability or duration of defenses will vary; some will be used and then quickly discarded, others will become stable and be built into the organization's routine. Where this happens to a defense, that is, where it becomes a stable part of the organization, it becomes a part of what can be called "organizational character." [12] By organizational character, I mean the organized total of all the stable, recurrent, defenses employed by a social system. In short, it is the cluster of methods commonly used by the group to cope with disorganizations. It is, in this sense, that the term "bureaucracy" best refers to a type of organizational character, rather than to a single defense mechanism; for when we inspect what it means, it can be seen to refer to a large variety of connected mechanisms; for example, it reduces tensions and conflicts by the integrated use of delimited spheres of authority and competence, formal rules, centralization, impersonal attitudes, and other devices.

---

[12] I believe that this notion was first used by Philip Selznick in his provocative, *TVA and the Grass Roots,* University of California Press, 1949, and later elaborated upon in his *Organizational Weapon,* McGraw-Hill, 1952. So far as I can judge, however, I have borrowed Selznick's term only, but not the way in which he employs it.

The career of a defense depends upon as large a number of factors, indeed frequently the same factors, as are involved in its selection. In the final analysis, the success or failure of a defense depends upon the "resistance" with which it is met, and the ability of those sponsoring the defense to overcome this resistance. This is another reason why the emergence of defenses is always problematical, and is never to be viewed with a mechanical optimism which assumes that for every threat there must arise some effective defense.

One of the important reasons why defenses are resisted is precisely because they may act *effectively* against some threat. It must be remembered that a threat is not a capricious, playful force. A threat is some system's defense, and as such, is anchored deeply in a social relationship; it is not likely, therefore, to be relinquished lightly. Actions against threats, defensive maneuvers, will, therefore, be resisted, because they are actions against some system's defenses[13]

Defenses against threats are, therefore, threats against defenses. Less paradoxically, defenses against threats to one system will act as threats against the defenses of another system. Since the defenses of one system are the threats of another, the more successful defenses are apt to be those which minimize their threatening aspect, or, as Harold Lasswell might say, "reduce provocation." An example of this may be found in the use of Ferdinand and Spiedman as scapegoats. Use of a scapegoat reduces provocation since it implies that the changes sought are minimal, and can be brought about with little alteration of organizational fundamentals.

This interplay between defense and threat can be illustrated by summarizing their role in the wildcat strike, which can be done in three basic "episodes."

Episode 1—Equilibrium: During and shortly after the war, labor-management relations were comparatively stable. The workers were producing according to the traditionalistic expectations of "Old Doug" who "didn't push the machine"; management was performing its role largely in accordance with the expectations involved in the indulgency pattern.

---

[13] By far the best codification of the concepts of "resistance" and "defense" is to be found in the fine article by Herbert E. Krugman, "The Role of Resistance in Propaganda," *International Journal of Opinion and Attitude Research,* Summer, 1949.

Episode 2—Disorganization and Defense: Changes took place in the market; it became harder to sell goods, harder to find jobs; Old Doug died. (*a*) These changes *threaten* management. (*b*) Management *defends* itself by initiating several successions to the plant management; Old Doug is replaced by Peele, and the latter by Landman. Management simultaneously introduces new machines, and other changes on the middle management level, the "strategic replacements." This new supervisory staff engages in closer supervision. (*c*) These *management* defenses in turn threatened the *workers*, violating their indulgency pattern in particular, and challenging their technologically-centered conception of their factory role. (*d*) The workers responded to these threats with their own variety of defenses, including aggression, apathy, and, finally, the wildcat strike. (*e*) These, in turn, threaten management, who feared for its control of the plant.

Episode 3—Development of Organizational Character: A compromise settlement was reached which, in effect, resolved the strike by increasing bureaucratic mechanisms. Possibilities of conflict were minimized by introducing rules which made explicit both parties' rights and obligations, and provided clearer standards for settling grievances. The plant was further centralized, the travelling engineer and stewards, both, were subjected to closer line control. The plant was restored to greater stability; overt conflict ended. This, however, was by no means a return to the situation as it had been; for, as a result of the defenses employed, the organizational character of the plant had been changed in a more bureaucratic direction.

The commitment to this organizational character did not, however, eliminate many of the tensions underlying the strike and, in fact, left open the possibility of their renewed expression. The organization's lines of communications had been lengthened; informal relations between workers and supervisors remained undeveloped; close supervision was eliminated only insofar as two of its foremost practitioners, Spiedman and Ferdinand, were concerned, but the apathy and resistance which could produce it in other foremen went unchanged; nothing was done to make supervisors more responsive to the workers' indulgency expectations. For these reasons, several weeks after the strike settlement, the workers began to talk again of another walkout.

In brief, the defensive measures which were agreed upon did not resolve the tensions, but initiated a vicious circle; they did not dissipate or eliminate the tensions, but caged them in. The development of a vicious circle is a crucial event in the career of a defense system. It developed here, largely because the people who had the greatest influence in shaping and selecting the defenses, namely the union officials and top Company management, focussed on those organizational needs which happened to coincide with their own status interests, and thus, for example, arranged to curtail the unsettling initiative of their own junior officers; but they failed to perceive that in doing so they impaired or neglected the requirements for the plant as a stable social system.

⸙ ⸙ ⸙

These, then, are rudiments of a general theory of group tensions. Such a theory is a strategic bridge between a "pure" sociology and an "applied" one; between a sociology whose central concerns are prediction or understanding, and one which searches for the step beyond this that can provide men with a guide to action in their time of trouble. The cumulative development of a general theory of group tensions is the first item on the scientific agenda of those seeking a "clinical sociology."

Revised November, 1964

harper torchbooks

HUMANITIES AND SOCIAL SCIENCES

American Studies

JOHN R. ALDEN: The American Revolution, 1775-1783.† *Illus.* TB/3011

BERNARD BAILYN: The New England Merchants in the Seventeenth Century TB/1149

RAY STANNARD BAKER: Following the Color Line: *American Negro Citizenship in the Progressive Era.‡ Illus. Edited by Dewey W. Grantham, Jr.* TB/3053

RAY A. BILLINGTON: The Far Western Frontier, 1830-1860.† *Illus.* TB/3012

JOSEPH L. BLAU, Ed.: Cornerstones of Religious Freedom in America. *Selected Basic Documents, Court Decisions and Public Statements. Revised and Enlarged Edition* TB/118

RANDOLPH S. BOURNE: War and the Intellectuals: *Collected Essays, 1915-1919.‡ Edited by Carl Resek* TB/3043

A. RUSSELL BUCHANAN: The United States and World War II. † *Illus.* Vol. I TB/3044; Vol. II TB/3045

ABRAHAM CAHAN: The Rise of David Levinsky: *a novel. Introduction by John Higham* TB/1028

JOSEPH CHARLES: The Origins of the American Party System TB/1049

THOMAS C. COCHRAN: The Inner Revolution: *Essays on the Social Sciences in History* TB/1140

T. C. COCHRAN & WILLIAM MILLER: The Age of Enterprise: *A Social History of Industrial America* TB/1054

EDWARD S. CORWIN: American Constitutional History: *Essays edited by Alpheus T. Mason and Gerald Garvey* TB/1136

FOSTER RHEA DULLES: America's Rise to World Power, 1898-1954.† *Illus.* TB/3021

W. A. DUNNING: Reconstruction, Political and Economic, 1865-1877 TB/1073

A. HUNTER DUPREE: Science in the Federal Government: *A History of Policies and Activities to 1940* TB/573

CLEMENT EATON: The Freedom-of-Thought Struggle in the Old South. *Revised Edition. Illus.* TB/1150

CLEMENT EATON: The Growth of Southern Civilization, 1790-1860.† *Illus.* TB/3040

HAROLD U. FAULKNER: Politics, Reform and Expansion, 1890-1900.† *Illus.* TB/3020

LOUIS FILLER: The Crusade against Slavery, 1830-1860.† *Illus.* TB/3029

EDITORS OF FORTUNE: America in the Sixties: *the Economy and the Society. 72 two-color charts* TB/1015

DIXON RYAN FOX: The Decline of Aristocracy in the Politics of New York.‡ *Edited by Robert V. Remini* TB/3064

LAWRENCE HENRY GIPSON: The Coming of the Revolution, 1763-1775.† *Illus.* TB/3007

FRANCIS J. GRUND: Aristocracy in America: *Jacksonian Democracy* TB/1001

ALEXANDER HAMILTON: The Reports of Alexander Hamilton.‡ *Edited by Jacob E. Cooke* TB/3060

OSCAR HANDLIN, Editor: This Was America: *As Recorded by European Travelers to the Western Shore in the Eighteenth, Nineteenth, and Twentieth Centuries. Illus.* TB/1119

MARCUS LEE HANSEN: The Atlantic Migration: 1607-1860. *Edited by Arthur M. Schlesinger, Sr.; Introduction by Oscar Handlin* TB/1052

MARCUS LEE HANSEN: The Immigrant in American History. *Edited with a Foreword by Arthur M. Schlesinger, Sr.* TB/1120

JOHN D. HICKS: Republican Ascendancy, 1921-1933.† *Illus.* TB/3041

JOHN HIGHAM, Ed.: The Reconstruction of American History TB/1068

† The New American Nation Series, edited by Henry Steele Commager and Richard B. Morris.
‡ American Perspectives series, edited by Bernard Wishy and William E. Leuchtenburg.
* The Rise of Modern Europe series, edited by William L. Langer.
|| Researches in the Social, Cultural, and Behavioral Sciences, edited by Benjamin Nelson.
§ The Library of Religion and Culture, edited by Benjamin Nelson.
Σ Harper Modern Science Series, edited by James R. Newman.
° Not for sale in Canada.

DANIEL H. HUNDLEY: Social Relations in our Southern States.‡ *Edited by William R. Taylor* TB/3058

HELEN HUNT JACKSON: A Century of Dishonor: *The Early Crusade for Indian Reform.‡ Edited by Andrew F. Rolle* TB/3063

ROBERT H. JACKSON: The Supreme Court in the American System of Government TB/1106

THOMAS JEFFERSON: Notes on the State of Virginia.‡ *Edited by Thomas Perkins Abernethy* TB/3052

JOHN F. KENNEDY: A Nation of Immigrants. *Revised and Enlarged Edition. Illus.* TB/1118

WILLIAM L. LANGER & S. EVERETT GLEASON: The Challenge to Isolation: *The World Crisis of 1937-1940 and American Foreign Policy* Vol. I TB/3054; Vol. II TB/3055

WILLIAM E. LEUCHTENBURG: Franklin D. Roosevelt and the New Deal, 1932-1940.† *Illus.* TB/3025

LEONARD W. LEVY: Freedom of Speech and Press in Early American History: *Legacy of Suppression* TB/1109

ARTHUR S. LINK: Woodrow Wilson and the Progressive Era, 1910-1917.† *Illus.* TB/3023

ROBERT GREEN McCLOSKEY: American Conservatism in the Age of Enterprise, 1865-1910 TB/1137

BERNARD MAYO: Myths and Men: *Patrick Henry, George Washington, Thomas Jefferson* TB/1108

JOHN C. MILLER: Alexander Hamilton and the Growth of the New Nation TB/3057

JOHN C. MILLER: The Federalist Era, 1789-1801.† *Illus.* TB/3027

PERRY MILLER: Errand into the Wilderness TB/1139

PERRY MILLER & T. H. JOHNSON, Editors: The Puritans: *A Sourcebook of Their Writings* Vol. I TB/1093; Vol. II TB/1094

GEORGE E. MOWRY: The Era of Theodore Roosevelt and the Birth of Modern America, 1900-1912.† *Illus.* TB/3022

WALLACE NOTESTEIN: The English People on the Eve of Colonization, 1603-1630.† *Illus.* TB/3006

RUSSEL BLAINE NYE: The Cultural Life of the New Nation, 1776-1801.† *Illus.* TB/3026

RALPH BARTON PERRY: Puritanism and Democracy TB/1138

RALPH BARTON PERRY: The Thought and Character of William James: *Briefer Version* TB/1156

GEORGE E. PROBST, Ed.: The Happy Republic: *A Reader in Tocqueville's America* TB/1060

WALTER RAUSCHENBUSCH: Christianity and the Social Crisis.‡ *Edited by Robert D. Cross* TB/3059

HEINRICH STRAUMANN: American Literature in the Twentieth Century. *Revised Edition* TB/1168

FRANK THISTLETHWAITE: America and the Atlantic Community: *Anglo-American Aspects, 1790-1850* TB/1107

TWELVE SOUTHERNERS: I'll Take My Stand: *The South and the Agrarian Tradition. Introduction by Louis D. Rubin, Jr.; Biographical Essays by Virginia Rock* TB/1072

A. F. TYLER: Freedom's Ferment: *Phases of American Social History from the Revolution to the Outbreak of the Civil War. Illus.* TB/1074

GLYNDON G. VAN DEUSEN: The Jacksonian Era, 1828-1848.† *Illus.* TB/3028

WALTER E. WEYL: The New Democracy: *An Essay on Certain Political and Economic Tendencies in the United States.‡ Edited by Charles Forcey* TB/3042

LOUIS B. WRIGHT: The Cultural Life of the American Colonies, 1607-1763.† *Illus.* TB/3005

LOUIS B. WRIGHT: Culture on the Moving Frontier TB/1053

Anthropology & Sociology

BERNARD BERELSON, Ed.: The Behavioral Sciences Today TB/1127

JOSEPH B. CASAGRANDE, Ed.: In the Company of Man: *20 Portraits of Anthropological Informants. Illus.* TB/3047

W. E. LE GROS CLARK: The Antecedents of Man: *An Introduction to the Evolution of the Primates.° Illus.* TB/559

THOMAS C. COCHRAN: The Inner Revolution: *Essays on the Social Sciences in History* TB/1140

ALLISON DAVIS & JOHN DOLLARD: Children of Bondage: *The Personality Development of Negro Youth in the Urban South* ‖ TB/3049

ST. CLAIR DRAKE & HORACE R. CAYTON: Black Metropolis: *A Study of Negro Life in a Northern City* Vol. I TB/1086; Vol. II TB/1087

CORA DU BOIS: The People of Alor. *New Preface by the author. Illus.* Vol. I TB/1042; Vol. II TB/1043

EMILE DURKHEIM et al.: Essays on Sociology and Philosophy: *With Analyses of Durkheim's Life and Work.* ‖ *Edited by Kurt H. Wolff* TB/1151

LEON FESTINGER, HENRY W. RIECKEN & STANLEY SCHACHTER: When Prophecy Fails: *A Social and Psychological Account of a Modern Group that Predicted the Destruction of the World* ‖ TB/1132

RAYMOND FIRTH, Ed.: Man and Culture: *An Evaluation of the Work of Bronislaw Malinowski* ‖ ° TB/1133

L. S. B. LEAKEY: Adam's Ancestors: *The Evolution of Man and his Culture. Illus.* TB/1019

KURT LEWIN: Field Theory in Social Science: *Selected Theoretical Papers.* ‖ *Edited with a Foreword by Dorwin Cartwright* TB/1135

ROBERT H. LOWIE: Primitive Society. *Introduction by Fred Eggan* TB/1056

R. M. MacIVER: Social Causation TB/1153

BENJAMIN NELSON: Religious Traditions and the Spirit of Capitalism: *From the Church Fathers to Jeremy Bentham* TB/1130

TALCOTT PARSONS & EDWARD A. SHILS, Editors: Toward a General Theory of Action: *Theoretical Foundations for the Social Sciences* TB/1083

JOHN H. ROHRER & MUNRO S. EDMONSON, Eds.: The Eighth Generation Grows Up: *Cultures and Personalities of New Orleans Negroes* ‖ TB/3050

ARNOLD ROSE: The Negro in America: *The Condensed Version of Gunnar Myrdal's* An American Dilemma TB/3048

HENRI DE SAINT-SIMON: Social Organization, The Science of Man, and Other Writings. ‖ *Edited and translated by Felix Markham* TB/1152

KURT SAMUELSSON: Religion and Economic Action: *A Critique of Max Weber's* The Protestant Ethic and the Spirit of Capitalism. ‖ ° *Trans. by E. G. French; Ed. with Intro. by D. C. Coleman* TB/1131

PITIRIM SOROKIN: Contemporary Sociological Theories. *Through the First Quarter of the Twentieth Century* TB/3046

MAURICE R. STEIN: The Eclipse of Community: *An Interpretation of American Studies.* TB/1128

SIR EDWARD TYLOR: The Origins of Culture. *Part I of "Primitive Culture."§ Introduction by Paul Radin* TB/33

SIR EDWARD TYLOR: Religion in Primitive Culture. *Part II of "Primitive Culture."§ Introduction by Paul Radin* TB/34

W. LLOYD WARNER & Associates: Democracy in Jonesville: *A Study in Quality and Inequality* TB/1129

W. LLOYD WARNER: A Black Civilization: *A Study of an Australian Tribe.* ‖ *Illus.* TB/3056

W. LLOYD WARNER: Social Class in America: *The Evaluation of Status* TB/1013

Art and Art History

WALTER LOWRIE: Art in the Early Church. *Illus. Revised Edition* TB/124

EMILE MÂLE: The Gothic Image: *Religious Art in France of the Thirteenth Century.§ 190 illus.* TB/44

MILLARD MEISS: Painting in Florence and Siena after the Black Death: *The Arts, Religion and Society in the Mid-Fourteenth Century. 169 illus.* TB/1148

ERICH NEUMANN: The Archetypal World of Henry Moore. *107 illus.* TB/2020

ERWIN PANOFSKY: Studies in Iconology: *Humanistic Themes in the Art of the Renaissance. 180 illustrations* TB/1077

ALEXANDRE PIANKOFF: The Shrines of Tut-Ankh-Amon. *Edited by N. Rambova. 117 illus.* TB/2011

JEAN SEZNEC: The Survival of the Pagan Gods: *The Mythological Tradition and Its Place in Renaissance Humanism and Art. 108 illustrations* TB/2004

OTTO VON SIMSON: The Gothic Cathedral: *Origins of Gothic Architecture and the Medieval Concept of Order. 58 illus.* TB/2018

HEINRICH ZIMMER: Myths and Symbols in Indian Art and Civilization. *70 illustrations* TB/2005

Business, Economics & Economic History

REINHARD BENDIX: Work and Authority in Industry: *Ideologies of Management in the Course of Industrialization* TB/3035

THOMAS C. COCHRAN: The American Business System: *A Historical Perspective, 1900-1955* TB/1080

ROBERT DAHL & CHARLES E. LINDBLOM: Politics, Economics, and Welfare: *Planning and Politico-Economic Systems Resolved into Basic Social Processes* TB/3037

PETER F. DRUCKER: The New Society: *The Anatomy of Industrial Order* TB/1082

ROBERT L. HEILBRONER: The Great Ascent: *The Struggle for Economic Development in Our Time* TB/3030

ABBA P. LERNER: Everybody's Business: *Current Assumptions in Economics and Public Policy* TB/3051

ROBERT GREEN McCLOSKEY: American Conservatism in the Age of Enterprise, 1865-1910 TB/1137

PAUL MANTOUX: The Industrial Revolution in the Eighteenth Century: *The Beginnings of the Modern Factory System in England* ° TB/1079

WILLIAM MILLER, Ed.: Men in Business: *Essays on the Historical Role of the Entrepreneur* TB/1081

PERRIN STRYKER: The Character of the Executive: *Eleven Studies in Managerial Qualities* TB/1041

PIERRE URI: Partnership for Progress: *A Program for Transatlantic Action* TB/3036

Contemporary Culture

JACQUES BARZUN: The House of Intellect TB/1051

JOHN U. NEF: Cultural Foundations of Industrial Civilization TB/1024

NATHAN M. PUSEY: The Age of the Scholar: *Observations on Education in a Troubled Decade* TB/1157

PAUL VALÉRY: The Outlook for Intelligence TB/2016

History: General

L. CARRINGTON GOODRICH: A Short History of the Chinese People. *Illus.* TB/3015

BERNARD LEWIS: The Arabs in History TB/1029

SIR PERCY SYKES: A History of Exploration.° *Introduction by John K. Wright* TB/1046

History: Ancient and Medieval

A. ANDREWES: The Greek Tyrants TB/1103

P. BOISSONNADE: Life and Work in Medieval Europe: *The Evolution of the Medieval Economy, the Fifth to the Fifteenth Centuries.° Preface by Lynn White, Jr.* TB/1141

HELEN CAM: England before Elizabeth TB/1026

G. G. COULTON: Medieval Village, Manor, and Monastery TB/1022

HEINRICH FICHTENAU: The Carolingian Empire: *The Age of Charlemagne* TB/1142

F. L. GANSHOF: Feudalism TB/1058

J. M. HUSSEY: The Byzantine World TB/1057

SAMUEL NOAH KRAMER: Sumerian Mythology TB/1055

FERDINAND LOT: The End of the Ancient World and the Beginnings of the Middle Ages. *Introduction by Glanville Downey* TB/1044

CHARLES PETIT-DUTAILLIS: The Feudal Monarchy in France and England: *From the Tenth to the Thirteenth Century* ° TB/1165

STEVEN RUNCIMAN: A History of the Crusades. Volume I: *The First Crusade and the Foundation of the Kingdom of Jerusalem. Illus.* TB/1143

FERDINAND SCHEVILL: Siena: *The History of a Medieval Commune. Introduction by William M. Bowsky* TB/1164

HENRY OSBORN TAYLOR: The Classical Heritage of the Middle Ages. *Foreword and Biblio. by Kenneth M. Setton* [Formerly listed as TB/48 under the title *The Emergence of Christian Culture in the West*] TB/1117

J. M. WALLACE-HADRILL: The Barbarian West: *The Early Middle Ages, A.D. 400-1000* TB/1061

History: Renaissance & Reformation

R. R. BOLGAR: The Classical Heritage and Its Beneficiaries: *From the Carolingian Age to the End of the Renaissance* TB/1125

JACOB BURCKHARDT: The Civilization of the Renaissance in Italy. *Introduction by Benjamin Nelson and Charles Trinkaus. Illus.* Volume I TB/40
Volume II TB/41

ERNST CASSIRER: The Individual and the Cosmos in Renaissance Philosophy. *Translated with an Introduction by Mario Domandi* TB/1097

EDWARD P. CHEYNEY: The Dawn of a New Era, 1250-1453.* *Illus.* TB/3002

DESIDERIUS ERASMUS: Christian Humanism and the Reformation: *Selected Writings. Edited and translated by John C. Olin* TB/1166

WALLACE K. FERGUSON et al.: Facets of the Renaissance TB/1098

WALLACE K. FERGUSON et al.: The Renaissance: *Six Essays. Illus.* TB/1084

MYRON P. GILMORE: The World of Humanism, 1453-1517.* *Illus.* TB/3003

FRANCESCO GUICCIARDINI: Maxims and Reflections of a Renaissance Statesman: *Ricordi. Trans. by Mario Domandi. Intro. by Nicolai Rubinstein* TB/1160

JOHAN HUIZINGA: Erasmus and the Age of Reformation. *Illus.* TB/19

ULRICH VON HUTTEN et al.: On the Eve of the Reformation: *"Letters of Obscure Men." Introduction by Hajo Holborn* TB/1124

PAUL O. KRISTELLER: Renaissance Thought: *The Classic, Scholastic, and Humanist Strains* TB/1048

PAUL O. KRISTELLER: Renaissance Thought II: *Papers on Humanism and the Arts* TB/1163

NICCOLÒ MACHIAVELLI: History of Florence and of the Affairs of Italy: *from the earliest times to the death of Lorenzo the Magnificent. Introduction by Felix Gilbert* TB/1027

ALFRED VON MARTIN: Sociology of the Renaissance. *Introduction by Wallace K. Ferguson* TB/1099

GARRETT MATTINGLY et al.: Renaissance Profiles. *Edited by J. H. Plumb* TB/1162

MILLARD MEISS: Painting in Florence and Siena after the Black Death. *The Arts, Religion and Society in the Mid-Fourteenth Century. 169 illus.* TB/1148

J. E. NEALE: The Age of Catherine de Medici° TB/1085

ERWIN PANOFSKY: Studies in Iconology: *Humanistic Themes in the Art of the Renaissance. 180 illustrations* TB/1077

J. H. PARRY: The Establishment of the European Hegemony: 1415-1715 TB/1045

HENRI PIRENNE: Early Democracies in the Low Countries: *Urban Society and Political Conflict in the Middle Ages and the Renaissance. Introduction by John Mundy* TB/1110

J. H. PLUMB: The Italian Renaissance: *A Concise Survey of Its History and Culture* TB/1161

FERDINAND SCHEVILL: The Medici. *Illus.* TB/1010

FERDINAND SCHEVILL: Medieval and Renaissance Florence. *Illus.* Volume I: *Medieval Florence* TB/1090
Volume II: *The Coming of Humanism and the Age of the Medici* TB/1091

G. M. TREVELYAN: England in the Age of Wycliffe, 1368-1520° TB/1112

VESPASIANO: Renaissance Princes, Popes, and Prelates: *The Vespasiano Memoirs: Lives of Illustrious Men of the XVth Century. Introduction by Myron P. Gilmore* TB/1111

History: Modern European

FREDERICK B. ARTZ: Reaction and Revolution, 1815-1832.* *Illus.* TB/3034

MAX BELOFF: The Age of Absolutism, 1660-1815 TB/1062

ROBERT C. BINKLEY: Realism and Nationalism, 1852-1871.* *Illus.* TB/3038

CRANE BRINTON: A Decade of Revolution, 1789-1799.* *Illus.* TB/3018

J. BRONOWSKI & BRUCE MAZLISH: The Western Intellectual Tradition: *From Leonardo to Hegel* TB/3001

GEOFFREY BRUUN: Europe and the French Imperium, 1799-1814.* *Illus.* TB/3033

ALAN BULLOCK: Hitler, A Study in Tyranny.° *Illus.* TB/1123

E. H. CARR: The Twenty Years' Crisis, 1919-1939: *An Introduction to the Study of International Relations°* TB/1122

GORDON A. CRAIG: From Bismarck to Adenauer: *Aspects of German Statecraft. Revised Edition* TB/1171

WALTER L. DORN: Competition for Empire, 1740-1763.* *Illus.* TB/3032

CARL J. FRIEDRICH: The Age of the Baroque, 1610-1660.* *Illus.* TB/3004

LEO GERSHOY: From Despotism to Revolution, 1763-1789.* *Illus.* TB/3017

ALBERT GOODWIN: The French Revolution TB/1064

CARLTON J. H. HAYES: A Generation of Materialism, 1871-1900.* *Illus.* TB/3039

J. H. HEXTER: Reappraisals in History: *New Views on History and Society in Early Modern Europe* TB/1100

A. R. HUMPHREYS: The Augustan World: *Society, Thought, and Letters in Eighteenth Century England* TB/1105

HANS KOHN, Ed.: The Mind of Modern Russia: *Historical and Political Thought of Russia's Great Age* TB/1065

SIR LEWIS NAMIER: Vanished Supremacies: *Essays on European History, 1812-1918°* TB/1088

JOHN U. NEF: Western Civilization Since the Renaissance: *Peace, War, Industry, and the Arts* TB/1113

FREDERICK L. NUSSBAUM: The Triumph of Science and Reason, 1660-1685.* *Illus.* TB/3009

RAYMOND W. POSTGATE, Ed.: Revolution from 1789 to 1906: *Selected Documents* TB/1063

PENFIELD ROBERTS: The Quest for Security, 1715-1740.* *Illus.* TB/3016

PRISCILLA ROBERTSON: Revolutions of 1848: *A Social History* TB/1025

ALBERT SOREL: Europe Under the Old Regime. *Translated by Francis H. Herrick* TB/1121

N. N. SUKHANOV: The Russian Revolution, 1917: *Eyewitness Account. Edited by Joel Carmichael*
Vol. I TB/1066; Vol. II TB/1067

JOHN B. WOLF: The Emergence of the Great Powers, 1685-1715.* *Illus.* TB/3010

JOHN B. WOLF: France: 1814-1919: *The Rise of a Liberal-Democratic Society* TB/3019

Intellectual History

HERSCHEL BAKER: The Image of Man: *A Study of the Idea of Human Dignity in Classical Antiquity, the Middle Ages, and the Renaissance* TB/1047

J. BRONOWSKI & BRUCE MAZLISH: The Western Intellectual Tradition: *From Leonardo to Hegel* TB/3001

ERNST CASSIRER: The Individual and the Cosmos in Renaissance Philosophy. *Translated with an Introduction by Mario Domandi* TB/1097

NORMAN COHN: The Pursuit of the Millennium: *Revolutionary Messianism in medieval and Reformation Europe and its bearing on modern Leftist and Rightist totalitarian movements* TB/1037

ARTHUR O. LOVEJOY: The Great Chain of Being: *A Study of the History of an Idea* TB/1009

ROBERT PAYNE: Hubris: *A Study of Pride. Foreword by Sir Herbert Read* TB/1031

BRUNO SNELL: The Discovery of the Mind: *The Greek Origins of European Thought* TB/1018

ERNEST LEE TUVESON: Millennium and Utopia: *A Study in the Background of the Idea of Progress.*|| *New Preface by the Author* TB/1134

Literature, Poetry, The Novel & Criticism

JAMES BAIRD: Ishmael: *The Art of Melville in the Contexts of International Primitivism* TB/1023

JACQUES BARZUN: The House of Intellect TB/1051

W. J. BATE: From Classic to Romantic: *Premises of Taste in Eighteenth Century England* TB/1036

RACHEL BESPALOFF: On the Iliad TB/2006

R. P. BLACKMUR et al.: Lectures in Criticism. *Introduction by Huntington Cairns* TB/2003

ABRAHAM CAHAN: The Rise of David Levinsky: *a novel. Introduction by John Higham* TB/1028

ERNST R. CURTIUS: European Literature and the Latin Middle Ages TB/2015

GEORGE ELIOT: Daniel Deronda: *a novel. Introduction by F. R. Leavis* TB/1039

ETIENNE GILSON: Dante and Philosophy TB/1089

ALFRED HARBAGE: As They Liked It: *A Study of Shakespeare's Moral Artistry* TB/1035

STANLEY R. HOPPER, Ed.: Spiritual Problems in Contemporary Literature§ TB/21

A. R. HUMPHREYS: The Augustan World: *Society, Thought, and Letters in Eighteenth Century England*[o] TB/1105

ALDOUS HUXLEY: Antic Hay & The Gioconda Smile.[o] *Introduction by Martin Green* TB/3503

HENRY JAMES: Roderick Hudson: *a novel. Introduction by Leon Edel* TB/1016

HENRY JAMES: The Tragic Muse: *a novel. Introduction by Leon Edel* TB/1017

ARNOLD KETTLE: An Introduction to the English Novel. Volume I: *Defoe to George Eliot* TB/1011
Volume II: *Henry James to the Present* TB/1012

ROGER SHERMAN LOOMIS: The Development of Arthurian Romance TB/1167

JOHN STUART MILL: On Bentham and Coleridge. *Introduction by F. R. Leavis* TB/1070

PERRY MILLER & T. H. JOHNSON, Editors: The Puritans: *A Sourcebook of Their Writings* Vol. I TB/1093
Vol. II TB/1094

KENNETH B. MURDOCK: Literature and Theology in Colonial New England TB/99

SAMUEL PEPYS: The Diary of Samuel Pepys.[o] *Edited by O. F. Morshead. Illus. by Ernest Shepard* TB/1007

ST.-JOHN PERSE: Seamarks TB/2002

O. E. RÖLVAAG: Giants in the Earth TB/3504

GEORGE SANTAYANA: Interpretations of Poetry and Religion§ TB/9

C. P. SNOW: Time of Hope: *a novel* TB/1040

HEINRICH STRAUMANN: American Literature in the Twentieth Century. *Revised Edition* TB/1168

DOROTHY VAN GHENT: The English Novel: *Form and Function* TB/1050

E. B. WHITE: One Man's Meat. *Introduction by Walter Blair* TB/3505

MORTON DAUWEN ZABEL, Editor: Literary Opinion in America. Vol. I TB/3013; Vol. II TB/3014

Myth, Symbol & Folklore

JOSEPH CAMPBELL, Editor: Pagan and Christian Mysteries. *Illus.* TB/2013

MIRCEA ELIADE: Cosmos and History: *The Myth of the Eternal Return*§ TB/2050

C. G. JUNG & C. KERÉNYI: Essays on a Science of Mythology: *The Myths of the Divine Child and the Divine Maiden* TB/2014

ERWIN PANOFSKY: Studies in Iconology: *Humanistic Themes in the Art of the Renaissance. 180 illustrations* TB/1077

JEAN SEZNEC: The Survival of the Pagan Gods: *The Mythological Tradition and its Place in Renaissance Humanism and Art. 108 illustrations* TB/2004

HELLMUT WILHELM: Change: *Eight Lectures on the I Ching* TB/2019

HEINRICH ZIMMER: Myths and Symbols in Indian Art and Civilization. *70 illustrations* TB/2005

Philosophy

HENRI BERGSON: Time and Free Will: *An Essay on the Immediate Data of Consciousness*[o] TB/1021

H. J. BLACKHAM: Six Existentialist Thinkers: *Kierkegaard, Nietzsche, Jaspers, Marcel, Heidegger, Sartre*[o] TB/1002

ERNST CASSIRER: The Individual and the Cosmos in Renaissance Philosophy. *Translated with an Introduction by Mario Domandi* TB/1097

ERNST CASSIRER: Rousseau, Kant and Goethe. *Introduction by Peter Gay* TB/1092

FREDERICK COPLESTON: Medieval Philosophy[o] TB/376

F. M. CORNFORD: From Religion to Philosophy: *A Study in the Origins of Western Speculation*§ TB/20

WILFRID DESAN: The Tragic Finale: *An Essay on the Philosophy of Jean-Paul Sartre* TB/1030

PAUL FRIEDLÄNDER: Plato: *An Introduction* TB/2017

ETIENNE GILSON: Dante and Philosophy TB/1089

WILLIAM CHASE GREENE: Moira: *Fate, Good, and Evil in Greek Thought* TB/1104

W. K. C. GUTHRIE: The Greek Philosophers: *From Thales to Aristotle*° TB/1008

F. H. HEINEMANN: Existentialism and the Modern Predicament TB/28

EDMUND HUSSERL: Phenomenology and the Crisis of Philosophy. *Translated with an Introduction by Quentin Lauer* TB/1170

IMMANUEL KANT: The Doctrine of Virtue, *being Part II of The Metaphysic of Morals. Translated with Notes and Introduction by Mary J. Gregor. Foreword by H. J. Paton* TB/110

IMMANUEL KANT: Groundwork of the Metaphysic of Morals. *Translated and analyzed by H. J. Paton* TB/1159

IMMANUEL KANT: Lectures on Ethics.§ *Introduction by Lewis W. Beck* TB/105

QUENTIN LAUER: Phenomenology: *Its Genesis and Prospect* TB/1169

JOHN MACQUARRIE: An Existentialist Theology: *A Comparison of Heidegger and Bultmann.*° *Preface by Rudolf Bultmann* TB/125

MICHAEL POLANYI: Personal Knowledge: *Towards a Post-Critical Philosophy* TB/1158

WILLARD VAN ORMAN QUINE: From a Logical Point of View: *Logico-Philosophical Essays* TB/566

BERTRAND RUSSELL et al.: The Philosophy of Bertrand Russell. *Edited by Paul Arthur Schilpp* Vol. I TB/1095; Vol. II TB/1096

L. S. STEBBING: A Modern Introduction to Logic TB/538

ALFRED NORTH WHITEHEAD: Process and Reality: *An Essay in Cosmology* TB/1033

WILHELM WINDELBAND: A History of Philosophy
Vol. I: *Greek, Roman, Medieval* TB/38
Vol. II: *Renaissance, Enlightenment, Modern* TB/39

Philosophy of History

NICOLAS BERDYAEV: The Beginning and the End§ TB/14

NICOLAS BERDYAEV: The Destiny of Man TB/61

WILHELM DILTHEY: Pattern and Meaning in History: *Thoughts on History and Society.*° *Edited with an Introduction by H. P. Rickman* TB/1075

RAYMOND KLIBANSKY & H. J. PATON, Eds.: Philosophy and History: *The Ernst Cassirer Festschrift. Illus.* TB/1115

JOSE ORTEGA Y GASSET: The Modern Theme. *Introduction by Jose Ferrater Mora* TB/1038

KARL R. POPPER: The Poverty of Historicism° TB/1126

W. H. WALSH: Philosophy of History: *An Introduction* TB/1020

Political Science & Government

JEREMY BENTHAM: The Handbook of Political Fallacies: *Introduction by Crane Brinton* TB/1069

KENNETH E. BOULDING: Conflict and Defense: *A General Theory* TB/3024

CRANE BRINTON: English Political Thought in the Nineteenth Century TB/1071

EDWARD S. CORWIN: American Constitutional History: *Essays edited by Alpheus T. Mason and Gerald Garvey* TB/1136

ROBERT DAHL & CHARLES E. LINDBLOM: Politics, Economics, and Welfare: *Planning and Politico-Economic Systems Resolved into Basic Social Processes* TB/3037

JOHN NEVILLE FIGGIS: Political Thought from Gerson to Grotius: 1414-1625: *Seven Studies. Introduction by Garrett Mattingly* TB/1032

F. L. GANSHOF: Feudalism TB/1058

G. P. GOOCH: English Democratic Ideas in the Seventeenth Century TB/1006

ROBERT H. JACKSON: The Supreme Court in the American System of Government TB/1106

DAN N. JACOBS, Ed.: The New Communist Manifesto *and Related Documents* TB/1078

DAN N. JACOBS & HANS BAERWALD, Eds.: Chinese Communism: *Selected Documents* TB/3031

KINGSLEY MARTIN: French Liberal Thought in the Eighteenth Century: *Political Ideas from Bayle to Condorcet* TB/1114

JOHN STUART MILL: On Bentham and Coleridge. *Introduction by F. R. Leavis* TB/1070

JOHN B. MORRALL: Political Thought in Medieval Times TB/1076

KARL R. POPPER: The Open Society and Its Enemies
Vol. I: *The Spell of Plato* TB/1101
Vol. II: *The High Tide of Prophecy: Hegel, Marx, and the Aftermath* TB/1102

HENRI DE SAINT-SIMON: Social Organization, The Science of Man, and Other Writings. *Edited and Translated by Felix Markham* TB/1152

JOSEPH A. SCHUMPETER: Capitalism, Socialism and Democracy TB/3008

Psychology

ALFRED ADLER: Problems of Neurosis. *Introduction by Heinz L. Ansbacher*|| TB/1145

ALFRED ADLER: The Individual Psychology of Alfred Adler. *Edited by Heinz L. and Rowena R. Ansbacher* TB/1154

ANTON T. BOISEN: The Exploration of the Inner World: *A Study of Mental Disorder and Religious Experience* TB/87

LEON FESTINGER, HENRY W. RIECKEN, STANLEY SCHACHTER: When Prophecy Fails: *A Social and Psychological Study of a Modern Group that Predicted the Destruction of the World* TB/1132

SIGMUND FREUD: On Creativity and the Unconscious: *Papers on the Psychology of Art, Literature, Love, Religion.*§ *Intro. by Benjamin Nelson* TB/45

C. JUDSON HERRICK: The Evolution of Human Nature TB/545

ALDOUS HUXLEY: The Devils of Loudun: *A Study in the Psychology of Power Politics and Mystical Religion in the France of Cardinal Richelieu*§° TB/60

WILLIAM JAMES: Psychology: *The Briefer Course. Edited with an Intro. by Gordon Allport* TB/1034

C. G. JUNG: Psychological Reflections TB/2001

C. G. JUNG: Symbols of Transformation: *An Analysis of the Prelude to a Case of Schizophrenia. Illus.* Vol. I TB/2009; Vol. II TB/2010

C. G. JUNG & C. KERÉNYI: Essays on a Science of Mythology: *The Myths of the Divine Child and the Divine Maiden* TB/2014

SOREN KIERKEGAARD: Repetition: *An Essay in Experimental Psychology. Translated with Introduction & Notes by Walter Lowrie* TB/117

JOHN T. McNEILL: A History of the Cure of Souls TB/126

KARL MENNINGER: Theory of Psychoanalytic Technique TB/1144

ERICH NEUMANN: Amor and Psyche: *The Psychic Development of the Feminine* TB/2012

ERICH NEUMANN: The Archetypal World of Henry Moore. *107 illus.* TB/2020

ERICH NEUMANN: The Origins and History of Consciousness Vol. I *Illus.* TB/2007; Vol. II TB/2008

C. P. OBERNDORF: A History of Psychoanalysis in America TB/1147

RALPH BARTON PERRY: The Thought and Character of William James: *Briefer Version* TB/1156

JEAN PIAGET, BÄRBEL INHELDER, & ALINA SZEMINSKA: The Child's Conception of Geometry ° TB/1146

JOHN H. SCHAAR: Escape from Authority: *The Perspectives of Erich Fromm* TB/1155

RELIGION

Ancient & Classical

J. H. BREASTED: Development of Religion and Thought in Ancient Egypt. *Introduction by John A. Wilson* TB/57

HENRI FRANKFORT: Ancient Egyptian Religion: *An Interpretation* TB/77

WILLIAM CHASE GREENE: Moira: *Fate, Good and Evil in Greek Thought* TB/1104

G. RACHEL LEVY: Religious Conceptions of the Stone Age *and their Influence upon European Thought. Illus. Introduction by Henri Frankfort* TB/106

MARTIN P. NILSSON: Greek Folk Religion. *Foreword by Arthur Darby Nock* TB/78

ALEXANDRE PIANKOFF: The Shrines of Tut-Ankh-Amon. *Edited by N. Rambova. 117 illus.* TB/2011

H. J. ROSE: Religion in Greece and Rome TB/55

Biblical Thought & Literature

W. F. ALBRIGHT: The Biblical Period from Abraham to Ezra TB/102

C. K. BARRETT, Ed.: The New Testament Background: *Selected Documents* TB/86

C. H. DODD: The Authority of the Bible TB/43

M. S. ENSLIN: Christian Beginnings TB/5

M. S. ENSLIN: The Literature of the Christian Movement TB/6

H. E. FOSDICK: A Guide to Understanding the Bible TB/2

H. H. ROWLEY: The Growth of the Old Testament TB/107

D. WINTON THOMAS, Ed.: Documents from Old Testament Times TB/85

Judaic Thought & Literature

MARTIN BUBER: Eclipse of God: *Studies in the Relation Between Religion and Philosophy* TB/12

MARTIN BUBER: Moses: *The Revelation and the Covenant* TB/27

MARTIN BUBER: Pointing the Way. *Introduction by Maurice S. Friedman* TB/103

MARTIN BUBER: The Prophetic Faith TB/73

MARTIN BUBER: Two Types of Faith: *the interpenetration of Judaism and Christianity*° TB/75

MAURICE S. FRIEDMAN: Martin Buber: *The Life of Dialogue* TB/64

FLAVIUS JOSEPHUS: The Great Roman-Jewish War, *with* The Life of Josephus. *Introduction by William R. Farmer* TB/74

T. J. MEEK: Hebrew Origins TB/69

Christianity: Origins & Early Development

AUGUSTINE: An Augustine Synthesis. *Edited by Erich Przywara* TB/335

ADOLF DEISSMANN: Paul: *A Study in Social and Religious History* TB/15

EDWARD GIBBON: The Triumph of Christendom in the Roman Empire *(Chaps. XV-XX of "Decline and Fall," J. B. Bury edition).*§ *Illus.* TB/46

MAURICE GOGUEL: Jesus and the Origins of Christianity.° *Introduction by C. Leslie Mitton*
Volume I: *Prolegomena to the Life of Jesus* TB/65
Volume II: *The Life of Jesus* TB/66

EDGAR J. GOODSPEED: A Life of Jesus TB/1

ADOLF HARNACK: The Mission and Expansion of Christianity *in the First Three Centuries. Introduction by Jaroslav Pelikan* TB/92

R. K. HARRISON: The Dead Sea Scrolls: *An Introduction*° TB/84

EDWIN HATCH: The Influence of Greek Ideas on Christianity.§ *Introduction and Bibliography by Frederick C. Grant* TB /18

WALTER LOWRIE: Art in the Early Church. *Illus. Revised Edition* TB/124

ARTHUR DARBY NOCK: Early Gentile Christianity and Its Hellenistic Background TB/111

ARTHUR DARBY NOCK: St. Paul° TB/104

F. VAN DER MEER: Augustine the Bishop: *Church and Society at the Dawn of the Middle Ages* TB/304

JOHANNES WEISS: Earliest Christianity: *A History of the Period A.D. 30-150. Introduction and Bibliography by Frederick C. Grant* Volume I TB/53
Volume II TB/54

Christianity: The Middle Ages and The Reformation

JOHANNES ECKHART: Meister Eckhart: *A Modern Translation by R. B. Blakney* TB/8

DESIDERIUS ERASMUS: Christian Humanism and the Reformation: *Selected Writings. Edited and translated by John C. Olin* TB/1166

G. P. FEDOTOV: The Russian Religious Mind: *Kievan Christianity, the tenth to the thirteenth centuries* TB/70

ÉTIENNE GILSON: Dante and Philosophy TB/1089

WILLIAM HALLER: The Rise of Puritanism TB/22

JOHAN HUIZINGA: Erasmus and the Age of Reformation. *Illus.* TB/19

DAVID KNOWLES: The English Mystical Tradition TB/302

JOHN T. McNEILL: Makers of the Christian Tradition: *From Alfred the Great to Schleiermacher* TB/121

A. C. McGIFFERT: Protestant Thought Before Kant. *Preface by Jaroslav Pelikan* TB/93

GORDON RUPP: Luther's Progress to the Diet of Worms° TB/120

Christianity: The Protestant Tradition

KARL BARTH: Church Dogmatics: *A Selection.* TB/95

KARL BARTH: Dogmatics in Outline TB/56

KARL BARTH: The Word of God and the Word of Man TB/13

WINTHROP HUDSON: The Great Tradition of the American Churches TB/98

SOREN KIERKEGAARD: Edifying Discourses. *Edited with an Introduction by Paul Holmer* TB/32

SOREN KIERKEGAARD: The Journals of Kierkegaard.° *Edited with an Introduction by Alexander Dru* TB/52

SOREN KIERKEGAARD: The Point of View for My Work as an Author: *A Report to History.*§ *Preface by Benjamin Nelson* TB/88

SOREN KIERKEGAARD: The Present Age.§ *Translated and edited by Alexander Dru. Introduction by Walter Kaufmann* TB/94

SOREN KIERKEGAARD: Purity of Heart TB/4

SOREN KIERKEGAARD: Repetition: *An Essay in Experimental Psychology. Translated with Introduction & Notes by Walter Lowrie* TB/117

SOREN KIERKEGAARD: Works of Love: *Some Christian Reflections in the Form of Discourses* TB/122

WALTER LOWRIE: Kierkegaard: *A Life* Vol. I TB/89; Vol. II TB/90

PERRY MILLER: Errand into the Wilderness TB/1139

PERRY MILLER & T. H. JOHNSON, Editors: The Puritans: *A Sourcebook of Their Writings* Vol. I TB/1093; Vol. II TB/1094

KENNETH B. MURDOCK: Literature and Theology in Colonial New England TB/99

F. SCHLEIERMACHER: The Christian Faith. *Introduction by Richard R. Niebuhr* Volume I TB/108; Volume II TB/109

F. SCHLEIERMACHER: On Religion: *Speeches to Its Cultured Despisers. Intro. by Rudolf Otto* TB/36

PAUL TILLICH: Dynamics of Faith TB/42

EVELYN UNDERHILL: Worship TB/10

G. VAN DER LEEUW: Religion in Essence and Manifestation: *A Study in Phenomenology. Appendices by Hans H. Penner* Vol. I TB/100; Vol. II TB/101

Christianity: The Roman and Eastern Traditions

THOMAS CORBISHLEY, S. J.: Roman Catholicism TB/112

G. P. FEDOTOV: The Russian Religious Mind: *Kievan Christianity, the tenth to the thirteenth centuries* TB/70

G. P. FEDOTOV, Ed.: A Treasury of Russian Spirituality TB/303

DAVID KNOWLES: The English Mystical Tradition TB/302

GABRIEL MARCEL: Homo Viator: *Introduction to a Metaphysic of Hope* TB/397

GUSTAVE WEIGEL, S.J.: Catholic Theology in Dialogue TB/301

Oriental Religions: Far Eastern, Near Eastern

TOR ANDRAE: Mohammed: *The Man and His Faith* TB/62

EDWARD CONZE: Buddhism: *Its Essence and Development.° Foreword by Arthur Waley* TB/58

EDWARD CONZE et al., Editors: Buddhist Texts Through the Ages TB/113

ANANDA COOMARASWAMY: Buddha and the Gospel of Buddhism. *Illus.* TB/119

H. G. CREEL: Confucius and the Chinese Way TB/63

FRANKLIN EDGERTON, Trans. & Ed.: The Bhagavad Gita TB/115

SWAMI NIKHILANANDA, Trans. & Ed.: The Upanishads: *A One-Volume Abridgment* TB/114

HELLMUT WILHELM: Change: *Eight Lectures on the I Ching* TB/2019

Philosophy of Religion

RUDOLF BULTMANN: History and Eschatology: *The Presence of Eternity* TB/91

RUDOLF BULTMANN AND FIVE CRITICS: Kerygma and Myth: *A Theological Debate* TB/80

RUDOLF BULTMANN and KARL KUNDSIN: Form Criticism: *Two Essays on New Testament Research. Translated by Frederick C. Grant* TB/96

MIRCEA ELIADE: The Sacred and the Profane TB/81

LUDWIG FEUERBACH: The Essence of Christianity.§ *Introduction by Karl Barth. Foreword by H. Richard Niebuhr* TB/11

ADOLF HARNACK: What is Christianity?§ *Introduction by Rudolf Bultmann* TB/17

FRIEDRICH HEGEL: On Christianity: *Early Theological Writings. Edited by Richard Kroner and T. M. Knox* TB/79

KARL HEIM: Christian Faith and Natural Science TB/16

IMMANUEL KANT: Religion Within the Limits of Reason Alone.§ *Introduction by Theodore M. Greene and John Silber* TB/67

JOHN MACQUARRIE: An Existentialist Theology: *A Comparison of Heidegger and Bultmann.*° *Preface by Rudolf Bultmann* TB/125

PIERRE TEILHARD DE CHARDIN: The Phenomenon of Man° TB/83

Religion, Culture & Society

JOSEPH L. BLAU, Ed.: Cornerstones of Religious Freedom in America: *Selected Basic Documents, Court Decisions and Public Statements. Revised and Enlarged Edition* TB/118

CHRISTOPHER DAWSON: The Historic Reality of Christian Culture TB/305

C. C. GILLISPIE: Genesis and Geology: *The Decades before Darwin*§ TB/51

WALTER KAUFMANN, Ed.: Religion from Tolstoy to Camus: *Basic Writings on Religious Truth and Morals. Enlarged Edition* TB/123

JOHN T. McNEILL: A History of the Cure of Souls TB/126

BENJAMIN NELSON: Religious Traditions and the Spirit of Capitalism: *From the Church Fathers to Jeremy Bentham* TB/1130

H. RICHARD NIEBUHR: Christ and Culture TB/3

H. RICHARD NIEBUHR: The Kingdom of God in America TB/49

RALPH BARTON PERRY: Puritanism and Democracy TB/1138

PAUL PFUETZE: Self, Society, Existence: *Human Nature and Dialogue in the Thought of George Herbert Mead and Martin Buber* TB/1059

WALTER RAUSCHENBUSCH: Christianity and the Social Crisis.‡ *Edited by Robert D. Cross* TB/3059

KURT SAMUELSSON: Religion and Economic Action: *A Critique of Max Weber's* The Protestant Ethic and the Spirit of Capitalism. || ° *Trans. by E. G. French; Ed. with Intro. by D. C. Coleman* TB/1131

ERNST TROELTSCH: The Social Teaching of the Christian Churches ° Vol. I TB/71; Vol. II TB/72

NATURAL SCIENCES AND MATHEMATICS

Biological Sciences

CHARLOTTE AUERBACH: The Science of Genetics Σ TB/568

A. BELLAIRS: Reptiles: *Life History, Evolution, and Structure. Illus.* TB/520

LUDWIG VON BERTALANFFY: Modern Theories of Development: *An Introduction to Theoretical Biology* TB/554

LUDWIG VON BERTALANFFY: Problems of Life: *An Evaluation of Modern Biological and Scientific Thought* TB/521

JOHN TYLER BONNER: The Ideas of Biology. Σ *Illus.* TB/570

HAROLD F. BLUM: Time's Arrow and Evolution TB/555

A. J. CAIN: Animal Species and their Evolution. *Illus.* TB/519

WALTER B. CANNON: Bodily Changes in Pain, Hunger, Fear and Rage. *Illus.* TB/562

W. E. LE GROS CLARK: The Antecedents of Man: *An Introduction to the Evolution of the Primates.*° *Illus.* TB/559

W. H. DOWDESWELL: Animal Ecology. *Illus.* TB/543

W. H. DOWDESWELL: The Mechanism of Evolution. *Illus.* TB/527

R. W. GERARD: Unresting Cells. *Illus.* TB/541

DAVID LACK: Darwin's Finches. *Illus.* TB/544

J. E. MORTON: Molluscs: *An Introduction to their Form and Functions. Illus.* TB/529

ADOLF PORTMANN: Animals as Social Beings.° *Illus.* TB/572

O. W. RICHARDS: The Social Insects. *Illus.* TB/542

P. M. SHEPPARD: Natural Selection and Heredity. *Illus.* TB/528

EDMUND W. SINNOTT: Cell and Psyche: *The Biology of Purpose* TB/546

C. H. WADDINGTON: How Animals Develop. *Illus.* TB/553

Chemistry

J. R. PARTINGTON: A Short History of Chemistry. *Illus.* TB/522

J. READ: A Direct Entry to Organic Chemistry. *Illus.* TB/523

J. READ: Through Alchemy to Chemistry. *Illus.* TB/561

Communication Theory

J. R. PIERCE: Symbols, Signals and Noise: *The Nature and Process of Communication* TB/574

Geography

R. E. COKER: This Great and Wide Sea: *An Introduction to Oceanography and Marine Biology. Illus.* TB/551

F. K. HARE: The Restless Atmosphere TB/560

History of Science

W. DAMPIER, Ed.: Readings in the Literature of Science. *Illus.* TB/512

A. HUNTER DUPREE: Science in the Federal Government: *A History of Policies and Activities to 1940* TB/573

ALEXANDRE KOYRÉ: From the Closed World to the Infinite Universe: *Copernicus, Kepler, Galileo, Newton, etc.* TB/31

A. G. VAN MELSEN: From Atomos to Atom: *A History of the Concept* Atom TB/517

O. NEUGEBAUER: The Exact Sciences in Antiquity TB/552

H. T. PLEDGE: Science Since 1500: *A Short History of Mathematics, Physics, Chemistry and Biology. Illus.* TB/506

GEORGE SARTON: Ancient Science and Modern Civilization TB/501

HANS THIRRING: Energy for Man: *From Windmills to Nuclear Power* TB/556

WILLIAM LAW WHYTE: Essay on Atomism: *From Democritus to 1960* TB/565

A. WOLF: A History of Science, Technology and Philosophy in the 16th and 17th Centuries.° *Illus.* Vol. I TB/508; Vol. II TB/509

A. WOLF: A History of Science, Technology, and Philosophy in the Eighteenth Century.° *Illus.* Vol. I TB/539; Vol. II TB/540

Mathematics

H. DAVENPORT: The Higher Arithmetic: *An Introduction to the Theory of Numbers* TB/526

H. G. FORDER: Geometry: *An Introduction* TB/548

GOTTLOB FREGE: The Foundations of Arithmetic: *A Logico-Mathematical Enquiry* TB/534

S. KÖRNER: The Philosophy of Mathematics: *An Introduction* TB/547

D. E. LITTLEWOOD: Skeleton Key of Mathematics: *A Simple Account of Complex Algebraic Problems* TB/525

GEORGE E. OWEN: Fundamentals of Scientific Mathematics TB/569

WILLARD VAN ORMAN QUINE: Mathematical Logic TB/558

O. G. SUTTON: Mathematics in Action.° *Foreword by James R. Newman. Illus.* TB/518

FREDERICK WAISMANN: Introduction to Mathematical Thinking. *Foreword by Karl Menger* TB/511

Philosophy of Science

R. B. BRAITHWAITE: Scientific Explanation TB/515

J. BRONOWSKI: Science and Human Values. *Illus.* TB/505

ALBERT EINSTEIN ET AL.: Albert Einstein: Philosopher-Scientist. *Edited by Paul A. Schilpp* Volume I TB/502 Volume II TB/503

WERNER HEISENBERG: Physics and Philosophy: *The Revolution in Modern Science* TB/549

JOHN MAYNARD KEYNES: A Treatise on Probability.° *Introduction by N. R. Hanson* TB/557

STEPHEN TOULMIN: Foresight and Understanding: *An Enquiry into the Aims of Science. Foreword by Jacques Barzun* TB/564

STEPHEN TOULMIN: The Philosophy of Science: *An Introduction* TB/513

G. J. WHITROW: The Natural Philosophy of Time° TB/563

Physics and Cosmology

DAVID BOHM: Causality and Chance in Modern Physics. *Foreword by Louis de Broglie* TB/536

P. W. BRIDGMAN: The Nature of Thermodynamics TB/537

P. W. BRIDGMAN: A Sophisticate's Primer of Relativity TB/575

A. C. CROMBIE, Ed.: Turning Point in Physics TB/535

C. V. DURELL: Readable Relativity. *Foreword by Freeman J. Dyson* TB/530

ARTHUR EDDINGTON: Space, Time and Gravitation: *An outline of the General Relativity Theory* TB/510

GEORGE GAMOW: Biography of PhysicsΣ TB/567

MAX JAMMER: Concepts of Force: *A Study in the Foundation of Dynamics* TB/550

MAX JAMMER: Concepts of Mass *in Classical and Modern Physics* TB/571

MAX JAMMER: Concepts of Space: *The History of Theories of Space in Physics. Foreword by Albert Einstein* TB/533

EDMUND WHITTAKER: History of the Theories of Aether and Electricity
Volume I: *The Classical Theories* TB/531
Volume II: *The Modern Theories* TB/532

G. J. WHITROW: The Structure and Evolution of the Universe: *An Introduction to Cosmology. Illus.* TB/504

Code to Torchbook Libraries:

TB/1+	: The Cloister Library
TB/301+	: The Cathedral Library
TB/501+	: The Science Library
TB/1001+	: The Academy Library
TB/2001+	: The Bollingen Library
TB/3001+	: The University Library

A LETTER TO THE READER

Overseas, there is considerable belief that we are a country of extreme conservatism and that we cannot accommodate to social change.

Books about America in the hands of readers abroad can help change those ideas.

The U. S. Information Agency cannot, by itself, meet the vast need for books about the United States.

You can help.

Harper Torchbooks provides three packets of books on American history, economics, sociology, literature and politics to help meet the need.

To send a packet of Torchbooks [*] overseas, all you need do is send your check for $7 (which includes cost of shipping) to Harper & Row. The U. S. Information Agency will distribute the books to libraries, schools, and other centers all over the world.

I ask every American to support this program, part of a worldwide BOOKS USA campaign.

I ask you to share in the opportunity to help tell others about America.

EDWARD R. MURROW
Director,
U. S. Information Agency

[*retailing at $10.85 to $12.00]

PACK

Dul
Coc
Zab
Dru ... rder
Fort ... nd the Society

PACK

Billi
Mov
B
Faul
Coc ... *ory of*
Ir
Tyle ... *the*
R

PACK

Han
Deg ... *America*
Prob ... *eville's America*
Alde
Wri ... -1763

You ... as recipient.
Sim ... money order.

HA
49 E

Packet I ☐ Packet II ☐ Packet III ☐

Please send the BOOKS USA library packet(s) indicated above, in my name, to the area checked below. Enclosed is my remittance in the amount of ____________ for ____________ packet(s) at $7.00 each.

_____ Africa _____ Latin America

_____ Far East _____ Near East

Name________________________________

Address______________________________

____

NOTE: This offer expires December 31, 1966.